Contents

Foreword | vi

Introduction | x

1. Origin Stories | 1
   Legal Ops Rises Above Tech Support | 4
   Siren Song of Legal Ops | 6
   Shaping a GenO Culture | 7
   The Frustrated Futurist | 9
   The Long and Winding Road | 12
   From Controversy to Conventional Wisdom | 14

2. Reshape the Headwaters: Law School—Vanderbilt Leads the Way for Legal Ops | 16
   Students Steered, Careers Deterred | 17
   Look Inward, Lawyer | 19
   Careerist, Opportunist, or Fatalist? | 20
   Legal Ops in Academia | 23
   Legal Ops as Competitive Advantage | 25

3. To Lawyer or Not to Lawyer—That Is the Question | 26
   Benefits of the Law Degree | 27
   Law: The Starting Point, Not the Endpoint | 29
   GenO Breaks Down Silos | 31
   Law-Smart—But Not a Lawyer | 32
   Limits of Lawyering | 33
   Notching the Early Win | 34
   GenO Rising | 36

4. Technocrat or Process Maven? | 38
   Leading with Technology | 40
   Learn What You Need to Know | 42
   GenO as Business Enabler | 43
   The Power of the Budget | 45
   Bringing the Budget to Life—Getting Funded | 46
   Beware the Previous Playbook | 47
   Making the Big Shift | 49
   Integrating Perspectives | 52
   Be Transparent About the Learning Curve | 53

5. Metrics, Measurements, and Management Controls | 55
   Slow Down to Speed Up | 56
   Where to Start? | 56
   'Quick Wins,' Nuanced Pace | 57
   Applying EQ to Metrics | 58
   The Metrics Corporate Tour | 60
   Testing Your Theory in the Workplace | 61
   Waste Management | 63
   Shining a Light on Your Skills | 64
   'Management Controls'—It's Not What You Think | 66
   Understand It to Automate It | 67

6. The Power Qualities | 69
   Part One—Personal Qualities to Be Mastered | 69
   Reinventing the CLOC Wheel | 70
   The Power Qualities and Skills of GenO Success | 72
   Quality 1: Empathy—the headwaters of power qualities | 73
   Quality 2: Patience—tough to practice, worth the effort | 76
   Quality 3: Kindness—being gentle with the truth | 79
   Quality 4: Pure intent—a communications foundation | 81
   Quality 5: Morale Maven—pumping up the players | 83
   Quality 6: Adaptability—be responsive to your environment | 86

7. The How-To Power Skills | 90
   Part Two—With these skills, you will be able to take action to move your initiative forward | 90
   Skill 7: Primary colors/large numbers—keep it simple | 92
   Skill 8: Lead from the back—letting the client take charge | 94
   Skill 9: Humble self-promotion—make sure your work is seen | 97
   Skill 10: Rapid decision-making—from speed bump to process accelerator | 100
   Skill 11: Consensus mindset—how to get there | 104
   Skill 12: Radical transparency—all cards face-up | 108

8. The Evolution Continues: GenO and Generalist Counsel— Inextricably Linked | 112
   It's Interdependence, Not Codependence | 113
   Not a 'Nice to Have,' but a 'Need to Have'—Quintessential Example: ESG | 115
   It's a Team Sport | 118

From 'Just Do It' to Mr. Commodore | 119
Back to School—in the Battlegrounds | 119
Breaking the Glass Injunction | 121
Follow the Yellow Brick Roads | 122
Mindset Reset | 124
Take—or Make—Opportunities for Growth | 125
Contracts Are Data—but Also Relationships | 127
Starting Legal Ops from Scratch | 129
Putting Hertz in the Driver's Seat | 130
Full Partnership in Business Outcomes | 131
Legal Training as CEO Requirement? | 133

9. Cautionary Tales | 134
You Will Trip—Keep Your Head Up, Knees Up, and Keep Moving | 136
'Grinding It Out' Is Often Overlooked As a Strategy | 137
Know Who You Are | 139
Play to Your Strengths | 140
Managing a Legal Ops Playbook … or Is It Playbooks? | 142
Credentialing Can Become a Curse … If You Let It | 143
Speed Bumps on the Road to Success | 148

10. Predictions—the Next 5 to 10 years | 150
Inevitability Born from Precedent | 151
Risk-Adjusted Value Creation Will Supercharge Legal Ops | 153
OK, OK, Let's Talk About AI | 154
The More Things Change, the More They … Change | 154
Ethics As the Foundation of Integrity—Legal Ops As Steward | 157
Let's Go Back to the Humans | 157
If You Want to Go Fast, Go Alone. If You Want to Go Far … | 158

Contributors | 161

Foreword

Prashant Dubey and I met almost a decade ago when we were both serving on the Alumni Board of Governors at the University of Chicago. We hit it off right away and shared some fun evenings, playing pool, sharing beverages, and talking about our families. Our friendship grew and eventually we settled into having periodic chats on Saturday mornings while we walked in nature, each in our respective cities, a continent apart.

It wasn't until a few months later that we both realized how much we had in common in our professional lives. Prashant had co-authored a book called *The Generalist Counsel: How Leading General Counsel Are Shaping Tomorrow's Companies.* His book outlined how General Counsel (GCs) have rapidly become strategic business enablers; essentially "business people that happen to be lawyers," and it chronicled stories of these leaders—leaders Prashant called "Generalist Counsel."

I had just published a book of my own, *Building an Outstanding Legal Team: Battle-Tested Strategies From a General Counsel.* Many of the same principles espoused in Prashant's book were also contained in mine.

One of the common threads in our books was that a successful Generalist Counsel needs to build an integrated team with both hard and soft skills. In my book, I wrote about how GCs need to ensure that their teams contain both subject matter experts, or "specialists," who focus on key legal and business risks, and legal "generalists," who focus principally on partnering with the business. Both our books make the point, quite deliberately, that successful GCs are strategic business enablers who build teams with leaders across both dimensions.

I have also often spoken about the need for GCs, when building their legal teams, to consider both "hardware" (operational, technical, financial, and legal aspects) and "software" (culture, diversity, and capabilities, including soft skills such as emotional and cultural intelligence, and curiosity). Prashant outlined some of the same themes in his *The Generalist Counsel*. These considerations have never been more important. In *GenO: The Rise of Legal Operations*, Prashant and Mike Haven put a big emphasis on highlighting these skills and qualities of successful Legal Ops professionals.

General Counsel are increasingly responsible for leading enterprise-wide contract management initiatives. The opportunities for digital transformation inherent in such a data-centric project must be tempered with the recognition that contracting is, as Prashant would say, also "a fundamentally human-centric endeavor." Legal Operations, which is a vital player in any successful contract management initiative, must possess both the hard skills needed to deploy the technology and establish the enterprise data frameworks, and the soft skills required to ensure that human beings find value in adopting the new systems and processes. It is the optimal balancing of these dimensions by skilled Legal Operations leaders that is critical to ensuring successful results and avoiding a trail of change management carnage.

Prashant and Mike believe that successful GCs stand on the broad shoulders of their Legal Operations leaders, and that the GC's success is inextricably linked to that of their Legal Operations team. I couldn't agree more. The stories in this book outlined this dynamic in detail.

Over the past several decades, as I have built my own legal teams, I have always made Legal Operations one of my initial hiring priorities, even before the profession had a name. These professionals were a diverse group. Some had law degrees and legal experience, while others had purely business, technical or operational backgrounds. In some cases, they had both! Many of the large transformation initiatives that I championed were led by my Legal Operations leaders. I cannot give them enough credit.

Many of the stories in *GenO: The Rise of Legal Operations* describe Legal Operations leaders who have transcended traditional notions of what the legal department exists to do, thereby allowing their GCs to achieve stature as strategic business enablers. In so doing, these leaders have themselves moved beyond the goal of mere operational efficiency and led a (r)evolution centered on the realization of strategic value.

Prashant and Mike's storytelling approach, which focuses on real people and experiences, makes their book both eminently insightful and thoroughly enjoyable. Their stories describe how some of the most important pioneers and leaders in the Legal Operations space have shaped their careers, while also outlining how the profession has evolved. They describe the culture of transparency and sharing that has come to characterize the Legal Operations community and detail how enterprise-wide initiatives are increasingly being led by Legal Operations leaders themselves. It is interesting to note the blend of hard and soft/power skills that these GenO professionals have honed, as they have journeyed through their careers, "making good trouble." Some of my own Legal Operations leaders are highlighted in the book—and I couldn't be more proud of them.

The moniker GenO, or Generation Operations, is appropriate. Today's Legal Operations leaders are true business enablers who increasingly allow GCs and their legal departments to be value creators as well as risk adjudicators.

I highly recommend this book to all my GC colleagues, Legal Operations leaders (those who have achieved GenO status as well as those aspiring to this level), my colleagues in functions that interact with Legal—the CFO, CRO, CMO, CHRO, CIO, and, yes ... even the CEO. I also recommend this book to lawyers in private practice who are trying to understand how to build more productive relationships with in-house legal departments (hint: work with GenO Legal Ops leaders). This will also be essential reading for my friends and colleagues in the service provider and technology companies that support legal departments. For many of them, understanding the drivers behind the continuing growth of the GenO community will be a prerequisite to success.

I am honored that Prashant and Mike have asked me to write this foreword. It has afforded me the opportunity to revisit some of the principles in my own book and validate that my experience is shared by others in the industry. Thank you, Prashant and Mike.

The Legal and Legal Operations communities will most certainly thank you, as well.

Bjarne P. Tellman
Senior Vice President and Deputy General Counsel
Aramco

Introduction

In 2016, the inaugural Corporate Legal Operations Consortium (CLOC) conference was held in San Francisco. More than 500 professionals attended a conference focused on a burgeoning domain where many didn't even have an official designation in their companies that properly represented their remit. It was an energizing gathering but left (one of) the authors wondering why these "birds of a feather" flocked together.

Shared demons can create unity just as easily as shared dreams. Legal Operations as a profession in 2016 represented Legal IT, facilities management, and management of administrative staff; but it was also the vehicle by which General Counsel could attain their rightful place at the business strategy table. How could there be such a wide spectrum of how Legal Operations manifested in corporate law departments? Perhaps introspecting about how law practice has evolved can provide some insight.

The canons of the law in English-speaking nations have historically evolved slowly, episodically, on a case-by-case basis. The law is not in a hurry to change. It does so with caution and, generally speaking, with multiple reviews in instances of landmark changes. Thus, in the courtroom, the law school classroom, and the sanctuary of the law firm office, the first order of business is to find out exactly what the law says and has said—not what it may say tomorrow.

The business environment stands as the exception to this rule. The business world is like a churning legal cauldron compared with the other lairs the law inhabits. Especially at the enterprise level, there has been increasing pressure over time to learn what the law does *not* say, what instances the law does *not* apply to, and how the body of law that governs certain activities can be interpreted and applied *after* an action has taken place rather than before.

This desire for an accelerated response from legal experts is nothing new. Ironically, the evolution of the in-house legal department helped to give it more credibility. For eons, most corporations retained outside law firms to handle the bulk of their "important" legal work. The in-house legal representative was generally viewed as somehow less than a lawyer, someone who hadn't made partner at the firm or finished some distance below the top of their law school class.

The necessity to "run everything by the lawyers" in those days meant sending the materials to the law firm, then waiting for what often seemed an eternity for a response. Often, the response was not the desired one, and further communications with outside counsel followed—also at the pace (and billable hour rate) set by the firm.

Then a cadre of major corporations took matters into their own hands. In part, they were concerned about the level of outside counsel's invoices. But in addition, they wished to have someone on site with whom they could quickly consult on a legal matter. Regulatory scrutiny on corporations was increasing, geopolitical turmoil increased legal risks in an increasingly "flat planet" economy, and governance of corporations by boards was influenced by activist investors who demanded transparency and *proactive* risk controls vs. reactive risk management. The demons needed to be identified and quashed. It was time to wrest control from law firms. Dangling corporate compensation packages, and promises of a rational lifestyle devoid of billable-hour targets, in front of senior members of the law firm succeeded in wooing them into the fold. True law departments began to appear throughout the business world.

With high-performing lawyers now on staff, the leadership team expected much more of the legal decision-making to happen internally—and for the turnaround time for a decision to shorten considerably. As the pace of transactions continued to accelerate, the law department found itself challenged. After all, they were still trained by their law schools to ignore deadlines when researching anything of import. But expectations for their performance had changed once they came aboard. They gave up pursuit of the billable hour and traded it for service level agreements. What???

They found themselves attempting to keep up, to perform due diligence in the breach, and to watch with anxiety as their words of caution were misinterpreted or outright ignored by those business units eager to "close the deal." Even as the in-house legal team ascended in prominence, it became increasingly siloed. The law department, rather than outside counsel, became the place where the sprint to the transactional finish line stalled, where legal documents were slowly birthed and even more slowly brought into the rest of the enterprise world. The legal department became known as the "Department of *No*," or, worse, the place where "deals went to die."

GenO is Born

Out of this breach emerged the profession of Legal Operations, or Legal Ops, as it is colloquially known. We refer to it here as Generation Operations, or GenO—the growing field of multidisciplinary professionals who understand how to apply the law to the breakneck pace of the deal. In particular, GenO Legal Ops professionals are ones who have transcended the roots of the profession, borne from the need for law department efficiency, and have become true business enablers—viewed as critical players in a company's quest to maximize revenue and profits while minimizing risk and accelerating cycle time.

The most fascinating part of this transcendence is the speed at which it occurred. Law practice in corporations evolved over decades—in comparison, Legal Ops went from transactional and tactical to strategic and indispensable ... seemingly overnight.

As such, inspired by the CLOC conference in 2016, Prashant Dubey crafted a book proposal that was fashioned after the style of *The Generalist Counsel*—stories of Legal Ops professionals who had experienced and driven this transcendence. It was accepted by a number of publishing houses, but Dubey got waylaid by some life-altering events that created the need for a reset. The book proposal was shelved.

Then in 2023, after a number of introspective and enthusiastic conversations about how the Legal Ops community has really become a necessary component of not just law departments but organizations overall, we (Prashant Dubey and Mike Haven) decided to partner on the book and bring it to life ... together.

Not only did this project benefit from our partnership (diverse viewpoints always improve a dialogue and work product), but the passage of time only strengthened the hypothesis formed in 2016—that the Legal Ops profession was rapidly becoming a foundational element of value creation in corporations. There were not only more stories, but the stories had a richness borne from large-scale disruptions such as a pandemic, an explosion of impactful legal technology that had become enterprise technology, the continued emergence of the GC as a strategic business enabler ... and, yes ... artificial intelligence.

In this book, we examine the evolution of the Legal Operations profession into Generation Operations, or "GenO," from its pioneer days to its 2024 status of a separate domain that provides the connective legal tissue among business departments designed to meet the demands of the modern enterprise. This is done through the stories of professionals who have successfully entered GenO.

We knew these professionals—or we thought we did. However, once we truly examined many dimensions of their stories, personal and professional, we learned a lot about their trials and tribulations, the uneven paths traveled, the joys of opportunities presented, and the halting heart for the ones overlooked. The humanity inherent in the relation of these stories can't be ignored. Yes, we are talking about a profession. However, we are talking about humans who occupy these roles, who have emotions, desires, fears, and triumphs. The true understanding of this profession is rooted in the humanness of the people we grew to know—much better than (we thought) we did. We hope you enjoy reading these stories as much as we enjoyed hearing them and memorializing them in this book.

This is an exciting time for GenO, for it has yet to fulfill its true destiny.

On a personal note, it is important to stipulate that co-authoring a book is difficult. Hectic schedules are just one challenge. The other is the need to focus on "pure intent." This means that as we progressed on this book, we each had to trust the other, know that each of us had pure intent in all our actions, and allow for each person's creative freedom to be fully invoked. We managed to do that and are both better for it. Our friendship also grew, and, as we complete this book and approach publication, we are excited about the future of our personal relationship as well as our professional relationship.

                        Peace

                        Prashant and Mike

1

Origin Stories

It's not necessary to have a legal background to be successful in the Legal Operations space. It's advantageous in some ways to know the language, the culture and the mindset of the lawyers that you're working with, but those are things that can be picked up by anyone that is willing to dedicate the time and effort.

STEVE HARMON, *COO and General Counsel, Elevate*
Co-Founder, Corporate Legal Operations Consortium[1]

In reviewing the origin stories of today's GenO Legal Operations (Legal Ops), what is more common is that the first cohort of individuals to become Legal Operations professionals certainly did not set out with that title in mind. Nor did they even imagine that the intersection of law, business, technology, and operations would become critical for companies striving to excel in the digital age. How could they? Legal Operations as a formal function did not exist when they were cutting their teeth professionally.

But before we tap into these true tales of self-discovery, let's take a moment to talk about the early evolution of Legal Operations. The profession moved as a similitude of the evolution of the General Counsel, albeit asynchronously.

As noted in our introduction, corporate lawyers were considered to be cut from a lesser cloth until early in the new millennium. But as the regulatory environment tightened up and the frequency and cost of litigation mounted, outside counsel bills

---
1. Unless otherwise noted, quotations are from interviews with identified interviewees.

started to get the attention of the CFO and CEO. Then, disruptors such as electronic discovery (eDiscovery) entered the arena. A major game-changer, electronic data production requests suddenly began to determine the outcome of litigation before the lawsuit set foot in a courtroom. There was also the basic need for a General Counsel to be a departmental manager, with budget management and people management responsibilities; an operator who didn't drive revenue but consumed resources, and often was perceived as a "necessary evil" who always had to justify their resource demands. In litigious organizations, the bigger challenge was to try and minimize budget surprises, since litigation and associated discovery made costs unpredictable. The GC needed someone to help them understand legal department resource consumption trends and then help manage the volatility.

Ruby Shellaway, Vice Chancellor, General Counsel, and University Secretary of Vanderbilt University, put it this way:

> I was initially appointed as interim GC. In order to show my peers on the leadership team of the university that I could hold the seat permanently, I, of course, needed to give them confidence that I could be the institution's primary risk manager, and have leadership presence to be on the executive team. But I also needed to demonstrate that I knew how to manage a department—[that I possessed] fundamental business skills that would give them confidence that the broad remit of a department with significant resources could be entrusted to me. I knew I needed help and turned to Susan Hackett, a tenured legal leader who was the GC of the Association of Corporate Counsel for over two decades, to help me find a Legal Operations leader. That's how I met Lizzie Shilliam, who has been indispensable in my quest to not only run a world class department but also be the businessperson lawyer that my peers expect.

Shellaway's anecdote describes perfectly what really changed the position of General Counsel from "chief risk adjudicator" to "strategic business enabler"; that General Counsel internalized the need to be "businesspersons that happen to be lawyers." Further, their peers on the executive team expected them to act as a peer businessperson, which made it incumbent on General Counsel to step outside the boundaries of the law department.

Peter Bragdon, Executive Vice President, Chief Administrative Officer, and General Counsel of Columbia Sportswear Company, described the dynamic in the following manner:

> I don't think you can be effective if you don't understand all aspects of the business. This is a difficult concept for many lawyers, particularly those in law firms. If you operate in a global manufacturing environment, this may mean that you need to understand the mechanics of manufacturing a product in China and shipping it to Italy in order to really do your job well.[2]

For Legal Operations, this meant that they also needed to step outside of the boundaries of the legal department; understand the core business of the organizations they served, the daily work of the stakeholders who relied on the legal department; and become strategic business enablers themselves ... so that their General Counsel could take their rightful place at the business strategy table. Interdependency? Undoubtedly.

The corporate legal department beefed up as leadership fought for tighter cost control. Contracts had once been viewed as the purview of Legal but had always touched multiple departments, and as the importance of contract data became more apparent, the expectation of Legal was to become the owner of a business process that previously had no obvious administrative/executive owner. This need to store, track, data-mine, and manage the lifecycle of contracts was yet another "disrupter" that led to the emergence of GenO.

---

2. Prashant Dubey and Eva Kripalani, *The Generalist Counsel: How Leading General Counsel Are Shaping Tomorrow's Companies* (New York: Oxford University Press, 2013), 60.

Legal Ops Rises Above Tech Support

At first, Legal Ops was postured as many things but often as tech support for the legal department. Its domain focus was interfacing with IT in supporting basic legal department technology needs such as eBilling, matter management, and document/knowledge management; helping fulfill the mission of commercial contract management and litigation; and providing the GC's office with the technology required to handle the ever increasing volume of work. All of this had to be done while trying to balance the needs of an often (age-)diverse legal team. Many legal teams were composed of long-tenured lawyers who were set in their ways as well as newly minted lawyers who were tech-savvy. Daily, Legal Ops needed to interface with IT to determine how to best support these diverse needs. So, even at birth GenO was not siloed, but embedded in the two departments.

As the stature of the legal department grew, so did that of Legal Ops. It was starting to become the connective tissue joining the many siloed departments of the enterprise, and the C-suite was noticing. As the General Counsel's role evolved from outsourcing to cost control to revenue and value preserver/generator, Legal Ops followed suit.

Sally Guyer, Global Chief Executive Officer, World Commerce & Contracting, through her enterprise contract management lens, explains the internal mindshift that took place and validated those corporations that, early on, invested in Legal Ops.

> Those who think of Legal Operations as simply preventing bad things from happening miss the fundamental piece of the function being a business enabler. Legal Ops, if done correctly, enables successful outcomes from the contracts that our business enters into. So if we want to be a strategic business partner, then we have to have a mindset shift, we have to shift from this preventive attitude to one of much greater optimism and how the legal team can participate in the delivery of successful outcomes.

Rethinking Legal Ops' role requires rethinking the significance of all those contracts floating around the enterprise, she says.

> Nobody likes to talk about contracts. Contracts get put in the proverbial drawer. Let's stop talking about them as legal weapons. Let's stop thinking about them as documents that sit in a drawer and only come out when things go wrong. We only need to refer to the contract when something bad happens. And we have to change that mindset, too.
>
> We have to recognize that contracts are these economic instruments. What we need to do is use contracts as operational guides to drive the successful outcomes that we aspire to in the first place, that have driven us to create the contract in the first place. So recognizing the multidisciplinary nature of contracts, and the contracting process, we need to make sure that we are designing that process and the documents—the instruments themselves—for the user community.

That's a very hefty expectation of a department that historically "reacted" to situations and was just starting to transition to a proactive, risk avoidance framework. Now the legal department was expected to "drive successful business outcomes?" Not surprisingly, with the rise of the legal department, GenO rose apace. Soon every department went looking for their resident Legal Operations experts to help them manage their contractual obligations—obligations that struck at the very heart of the corporate bottom line.

But what sort of folks were led into these uncharted corporate waters as Legal Ops evolved? While most of that first group had legal training, some did not. In a sense, the profession found them—rather than the other way around. However, they were all looking for new challenges, either within the legal profession or in their evolving corporate careers (or both). So the paths taken to Legal Ops were as numerous as the members of this cohort.

Because there is still no conventional route to the Legal Operations function of most corporations, we believe the best way to tell this is to show it through the individuals who carved out the niche.

Siren Song of Legal Ops

Tommie Tavares-Ferreira, who runs the Legal Operations function at Cedar Cares, Inc., a FinTech firm, carved out a particularly circuitous route to Legal Ops—but all of her stops happened in New York City. And all of them involved contracts of one sort or another. She has also made a significant contribution to her chosen profession outside of her day job.

By the way, Tavares-Ferreira is not a lawyer.

> I started my career in the music industry at an independent record label. I was basically what you'd call today the chief of staff to the CEO. And so it was such a small place, that if we were signing bands or going on tour, the person who raised their hand and said, "I'll go figure out how to take a contract template off the internet and utilize it for the band," or "I'll go on tour with them," or "I'll go to the P.O. box on Prince Street and I'll go get our mail and fill these T-shirt orders" just did that thing. It was kind of that sort of scenario. It was the late '90s, early 2000s, and you have these DIY record labels coming and popping up.
>
> And I learned a lot about that entrepreneurial spirit there. It really was a figure-out-what-you-want-to-learn environment. If you don't know how to do it, kind of figure it out. That is not only such a part of Legal Operations, but such a part of who I am.

Her first official legal role was with record label giant EMI, as a digital paralegal.

> That was the time when all of the record companies were fighting with Napster. And look at how far we've come with streaming services just being a part of our day-to-day life. But back in the day, we used to actually fight over that kind of thing. And I

would write cease-and-desist letters and sort of started getting into what you'd call the legal side of the business there. I was getting into the contracts and the way that that department was running, almost as a paralegal. And that translated into a music-licensing role where I learned a ton about brokering deals for musicians who were licensing their music. And again, the back end of that business is a contract.

Little did she know she was on a collision course with a future as a GenO convert.

The leap wasn't immediate. Tavares-Ferreira continued to draft, negotiate, and manage contracts, but the stakes got higher, the deals more complex, her responsibilities—and need for a broader remit—ever increasing.

I was in a role where I really had a lot of empowerment, and a high volume of contracts, and a high volume of negotiations, something like 1,300 NDAs [nondisclosure agreements] a year. This was an order of magnitude greater than what I was used to. I realized very quickly, "We have to operationalize this."

Introduced to Legal Ops by a supportive General Counsel boss, Tavares-Ferreira admits she had not previously been aware that Legal Operations existed as its own domain.

So I come into a role I didn't even know existed, but yet someone is telling me I'm doing it. A Legal Operations passion was born in me in that role as a contract manager. And from there, the world has changed for me—this wonderful world I now live in.

Shaping a GenO Culture

Steve Harmon is currently the Chief Operating Officer and General Counsel of Elevate. Elevate is a law company, and a major contributor in helping law departments and firms implement practical ways to improve efficiency, quality, and outcomes. Prior to Elevate, Harmon was at Cisco Systems for nearly 20 years. This is where he shaped one of the industry's first comprehensive Legal

Operations teams, which became the training ground for a lot of Legal Operations leaders in our industry. So essentially, Harmon was doing Legal Operations before it was a thing.

He's also a co-founder and former board member of the Corporate Legal Operations Consortium (CLOC). He is very much a supporter of promoting industry collaboration among in-house Legal Operations professionals.

When Harmon graduated from law school, he didn't go into the practice of law. He actually started in a very nontraditional role. It was venture capital.

> In the summer between my second and third year of law school, I accepted an internship at a well-known network technology company called Novell, where I was focusing my practice on supporting the transactional licensing team at Novell. My undergraduate education was in electrical engineering and information systems, so I had a technical background that enabled me to look at the product sets that Novell was selling and figure out ways to support that legally. I was eventually introduced to our venture capital function. At the end of my internship, the general counsel invited me to join Novell as an employee. He said, "You can join as a member of our legal department, or we'd be happy to have you supporting the leader of our venture capital [VC] fund." It was a unique opportunity to marry the combination of my technical background and my legal background, all with the focus on network effects. I said yes to the VC job.

This was a unique position that catapulted Harmon into a world where finance, business, and law intersected, and where he focused on creating exponential business value for the company. On the back of this experience, Harmon eventually obtained a position with one of the fastest growing technology companies in the world, Cisco, where he worked for the General Counsel Mark Chandler, who took a very innovative approach to legal practice at the time.

Mark was very committed to the idea that the sole reason a legal department exists in an in-house environment is to enable the business. The mission statement that we used for the legal department was that the "department exists to enable the business to design, build, and sell its products in a legally appropriate way." Mark observed that, oftentimes, like many support functions within an organization, the legal department is viewed as a tax on the profitability of the business. It slows things down. Lawyers, by their very nature, tend to be risk averse. But Mark's approach was different. He reminded us on a very regular basis that the only way our salaries got paid is because the organization was designing, building and selling products. We certainly needed to do that in a legally appropriate way, and that was the nuance that we brought and contributed to every conversation. So every operation, every task that we took on within the legal department, was designed to enable the business in some way.

That became the mental mindset that I grew up with as a lawyer, essentially, to really focus on ways that the legal department could assist the business. And a lot of times that represented itself in challenges around optimization, figuring out ways to support the business with the least amount of friction as possible. And a lot of that was directed at reducing contracting cycle times. So, my Legal Operations journey really started with a specific effort to reduce contracting cycle times, and I relied on some of my technical background to help make that happen.

The Frustrated Futurist

In the early days of the emergence of Legal Operations departments, some were developed planfully as a natural bridge between Legal and the various business departments. But others evolved almost out of frustration. That was the case for Lizzie Shilliam.

Now the head of Vanderbilt University's Legal Operations team, Shilliam made her way to Legal Ops by identifying, and then filling, a gaping hole in Nike, Inc.'s contracting processes.

We started our contract management process at Nike because I had brought up to our CFO that we had risk in not knowing where all of our contracts were. I was on the procurement team at that time and we couldn't find contracts. They were in drawers, people had saved them to their hard drives, they were in all sorts of places. We found some very funny things. One lady told me she had the contracts secured, and I asked where they were. She said, "They're in a box in the back of my car, and at least I always have them with me." So that subject was a hot potato risk for quite a while. Nike was a $20 billion public company.

Shilliam penned a memo that got passed around to quite a few different departments, and the risk was brought to the attention of the board of Nike. The board agreed action to address the challenge was warranted. As with all such things that create risk in a company, the task of seeking a solution landed on the desk of the General Counsel. The GC, Hilary Krane, knew what she didn't know, and serendipitously met Shilliam and brought her into the legal department. So the task got handed down to Shilliam. But first, Shilliam had to get departmental buy-in throughout Nike, which was no small trick.

> Just because the board said to do it, it doesn't always mean that everybody automatically participates—especially in a company with many former high-level athletes in charge. So we went door-to-door talking to directors, talking to senior directors, asking them where their contracts were.

> Finally, with the support of our General Counsel, Hilary Krane, the CFO called me into his office one day and said, "Well, you started this mess, let's clean it up." He gave me a large budget and he also gave me headcount to hire, and consultants to hire, to figure out contract management at Nike and to put a global solution in place.

> I learned about how Nike operated prior to this contract management system and that the benefits of the system would really outweigh all of the selected ways that people were sav-

ing their contracts. They had their own system for sure, but it really didn't benefit the enterprise, especially being a global company and as large as they were and are today. They needed that global contract management system.

Thus was birthed Nike's Legal Operations function. In the process of identifying the problem and crafting a solution, Shilliam gained vital knowledge about Nike's widespread business operations that would serve her fledgling department well.

I started with one brilliant attorney, Genaro Lopez, and Genaro and I really worked hand in hand to identify best practices. They [lawyers who wanted to do this type of work] were much harder to find then—we had to create some of our own, because there was really no roadmap for this kind of process.

The work was tedious and grueling. But the objective—for one group to be able to manage the contracts of all the groups—was so enticing that they persevered.

We started going door-to-door, and pretty soon we realized that if we were going to look at all of these contracts and put a system in place, number one, we had to find all of the contracts per department. That was a huge project. But the second one was we had to extract the metadata from those contracts to make it useful in the system itself.

Knowing where a contract resided was beneficial. But the true power resided in having ready access to what the contract's obligations were for all parties. Guidelines had to be created to master the welter of data contained in the mountains of contracts.

It was really important to have a holistic view of the types of contracts that we were putting into the system. We had to decide whether anything was going to be excluded, and if so, why it was going to be excluded. We had to come up with a nomenclature for all of them, so we would have some sort of standards in the contract management system.

But who would do the actual work? That was Shilliam's next step—to build a team of players that would be excited about being part of a new internal venture.

> So we put together a team of attorneys that had decided they didn't want to go down the traditional path of law, and they were a fantastic group; a lot of Lewis and Clark College grads, others that we found around the Portland area. And with that team, we put together a contract management center of excellence that drove that contract management process throughout the organization. Our reach was global, and we did a lot of road trips around the globe during that project. It became just a way of life, not just for the legal department, but also for each department. Business units had a defined process to upload their contracts, get them through the legal department, and make sure that we did have best-in-class contract management.

If this story sounds like it just took shape one day at a time, we have properly represented the situation. The takeaway here is that Legal Ops is often formed when a pernicious business challenge arises and there is no obvious person to own the solution. Shilliam is one of myriad examples of GenO professionals who stepped up when they saw a challenge, didn't really know the solution, but plowed forward anyway. This takes courage and confidence ... and, yes, a certain chutzpah. If you haven't met Shilliam, we hope you do someday. The chutzpah ... it's still there! Just be careful if you challenge her to a game of pool.

The Long and Winding Road

Had Bob Mignanelli believed in following a fully charted career path to the top, he likely never would have landed where he is today: VP, Legal Strategy/Operations, Digital & Technology, & Procurement for Haleon (formerly GSK Consumer Health, maker of brands such as Theraflu, Advil, Emergen-C, Tums, and ChapStick). Mignanelli likes to keep his options open, though; he looks for opportunities for advancement, even ones that may look at first like side trips. No wonder he was among the lawyers minted in the pre-millennium days who found his way to Legal Ops.

He started working in a small law practice in Washington, D.C., soon after law school.

> It was a small firm. We did a variety of different things, but it was really around litigation and providing services to small-business clients. So that was my first introduction into two worlds. One was the pure legal side of it, but that world gave me a window into the other world: businesses, and how they are run, what's important to business owners. Although it was on a small scale, it taught me a lot of lessons there.

Mignanelli got the itch to go West. Relocating to Arizona, he told himself he'd do desert duty for a couple of years and then return to his stomping grounds back East. Two years turned into two decades, as Mignanelli found himself carving out a legal operations career. He landed a legal gig as a contracts manager at Pearson, the massive learning corporation, in the Phoenix area in 2001.

> I had pivoted and I was looking to join a corporation. So I took this role as a contracts manager at Pearson, which was fantastic, because it gave me an insight into how the business generated revenue, how it operated its business. I think people, when they talk about contracts work, or contracts management, and building contracting centers of excellence, they don't realize that all of that work is the lifeblood of the company. All of your business transactions are contained in those contracts, whether it's generating revenue, whether it's procurement, direct or indirect materials or services. All of that is embodied in the work that we're doing that really helps drive the business.

Within Pearson, Mignanelli moved from role to role as he cemented the marriage between legal and business.

That contracts manager role evolved into me becoming the corporate counsel for a number of Pearson's technology business units over the years. And if you think about what we do as in-house counsel, most of the advice and guidance I provide is around business terms, it's around commercial terms, it's around business strategy. And of course there's a legal overlay to all of that, because you want to make sure that the company's not going to do anything that will materially jeopardize its reputation, its financial assets, its position in the marketplace.

At Pearson, he joined forces with a true changemaker. Bjarne Tellmann came on as Pearson's general counsel in 2014, and the formation of Legal Operations accelerated. Under Tellmann's visionary leadership, Legal Operations became an indispensable adjunct to every department in the company. Mignanelli's focus on the technology side of contract management helped demonstrate to the rest of the corporation that Legal Ops had the tools to drive efficiencies in contract management, freeing up personnel in other departments to focus more on their jobs and less on the contracts that underpinned their work.

Mignanelli rose to Senior Vice President and COO, Legal and Associate General Counsel, Technology and Operations. Having built their legal juggernaut over eight years together at Pearson, Tellmann and Mignanelli moved on to Haleon in 2022 to reinvent the legal realm there.

> I've had an interesting path to where I am today, and something I have learned: Our paths are never straight lines.

From Controversy to Conventional Wisdom

These are but a few of the legal operations pioneers who had the vision, the courage, and the desire to reshape the corporate landscape by carving out an entirely new discipline. We say "courage" because they truly followed the beat of a different drummer. Those who went to law school eschewed the sanctioned legal career paths laid out to them there—after learning out in the working world that they didn't fit as cogs in stuffy, hide-bound law firms, or even with scrappy litigation houses. Those who invented Legal

Ops roles for themselves within the context of a corporate job had to fight for recognition and respect internally with essentially no prototype to point to for credibility.

Yet today they have shifted from career innovators to corporate changemakers. Their domain: the myriad interstices within the corporate body impacted by contracts and negotiated agreements of all sorts that, mycelia-like, flow throughout the enterprise, stitching it together in a web of legal threads.

This is where Legal Ops lives. This is where it works its magic. Often unheralded, the fluid management of all those bits and bytes of legal bindings has come to be recognized by the C-suite as an indispensable function within the corporate framework. Legal Ops is rising. And more savvy professionals are rising with it.

In a July 2022 article for the Penn Carey Law School of the University of Pennsylvania, attorney Lourdes M. Fuentes, founder of Karta Legal LLC, discusses the rise of Legal Ops and the critical role it plays in corporate success.

> The idea of elevating legal ops to the status of legal advice may sound controversial, but it is simply common sense in today's world. Indeed, we could author an entire thesis about why having the best Legal Operations team acting as the right hand to the best practitioners is the goal.[3]

If that is indeed the goal, how does one get there? If one looks for a law school experience as part of the pathway, the choices remain limited. But such schools do exist.

---

3. Lourdes M. Fuentes, "Elevating Legal Operations to the Status of Legal Advice," University of Pennsylvania Carey Law School, July 1, 2022, www.law.upenn.edu/live/news/14942-elevating-legal-operations-to-the-status-of-legal.

2

Reshape the Headwaters: Law School—Vanderbilt Leads the Way for Legal Ops

The irony is, these systems we've designed that serve lawyers so well do not serve us well as humans.

CAITLIN MOON, *Vanderbilt University Law School*

Caitlin Moon is on a mission to change the way law schools produce lawyers.

Moon, the Director of Innovation Design, Program on Law & Innovation at Vanderbilt University Law School, came to academia through law. Her career was nontraditional. She was among those who, early on in her career as a lawyer, identified herself as a member of the GenO profession. When Vanderbilt recruited her to teach at the law school, she recognized the opportunity to be a changemaker.

It was Moon's opinion that the legal profession—and, by extension, law school—was failing both lawyers and those they were supposed to be serving. She can cite the evidence, including more law school grads gravitating to corporate life and abandoning civil law; and much higher rates of depression, substance use, suicide, and career frustration among lawyers than the rest of the population.

When folks say "We can't change things"—that's a choice. Yes, we can. You just choose to—or not to. All the data is screaming that, if we don't change, we are looking at cataclysmic failure for pretty much everyone.

Students Steered, Careers Deterred

The trouble, she believes, begins with law school. Historically, students were not seen as people first and then as emerging lawyers, but simply as legal raw material. No one was asking them what they really wanted to do with their lives.

And their choices were limited. Because most law schools are traditionalists, law is learned through an agreed-upon curriculum that emphasizes certain paths—partner in a law firm, corporate counsel, public positions (public defender, prosecutor, judge), legal negotiators (labor-management lawyers, talent agents, arbitrators). Little attention is paid to other career paths, such as Legal Operations. In fact, at most schools, "new" legal careers are met with skepticism and ridicule.

Sally Guyer, Global Chief Executive Officer for World Commerce & Contracting, says law schools need to rethink their role in the lives of their students and those they will serve. Guyer, an early drinker of the Legal Ops Kool-aid, points out a key personality feature of successful Legal Ops professionals: an optimism about what happens when they do their job well. But optimism is not necessarily a viewpoint nurtured by law schools.

> The contract law modules that we learn at law school are all about things that go wrong. It's all about case law. And so we're naturally conditioned as students to think about the things that go wrong and to assume that our role is to protect bad things from happening to our organization. I'm not suggesting that that's not part of the role. Of course it is, but it misses the fundamental piece of being a business enabler, of enabling successful outcomes from the contracts that our

business enters into. So if we want to be a strategic business partner, then we have a mindset shift, we have to shift from this preventive attitude to one of much greater optimism and how the legal team can participate in the delivery of successful outcomes.

Reading between the lines of Guyer's conclusions, it appears law schools are pumping out newly minted lawyers who've been steered onto a career track that may well grind against their very essences. Perhaps worried about student debt, they may initially be drawn to a paycheck rather than a calling. This short-sighted decision-making—complicated by a lack of life experience—too often leads to years of misery. The misplaced person inside the lawyer's suit struggles to perform duties foreign to their nature. The beginnings of a recovering lawyer …

The consequences are all too real for another party in the legal system: those who desperately need legal assistance. Moon cites a recent study that found that just 8% of the legal matters for low-income people who need legal assistance get legal help. Even middle-class clients are only marginally better served.

Lawyers are harmed as well by the existing system, Moon says: Another study reported that those in the legal profession report substance-use difficulties and depression at three times the rate of the rest of the population.

> The irony is, these systems we've designed that serve lawyers so well do not serve us well as humans. When folks say, "We can't change this because it works"—it's not working for the vast majority of everyone in the system. It's not working for the people doing the work, and it's not working for the people we're supposed to be serving. So that's bullshit to say that it's working!

Straight talk. That's what one gets from Moon.

Look Inward, Lawyer

Given free rein to create her own department, Moon has crafted, over seven years, a curriculum based upon human-centered design. Moon did not invent human-centered design (HCD). But she has certainly tweaked it for Vanderbilt students. Essentially, HCD encourages students to go inward, find out who they really are, and then consider what sort of legal future might best fit their personalities. Pretty much the opposite of traditional law school training.

In a few short years, Moon's classes became wildly popular, as they awakened students to who they really were and how that knowledge could serve them as they moved toward a career in law.

> My focus of teaching is to help students figure out how we make law better, how we make the delivery of legal services better. We focus on legal services delivery. It's a fabulous playground for me, because I get to focus on and think about what are those skills and ideas and themes that we need to focus on for our law students as they prepare to enter the legal world.

Meanwhile, Vanderbilt University hired Lizzie Shilliam, another GenO pioneer, as VP Legal Operations & Chief of Staff of the Office of General Counsel. In time she met Moon, and they clicked. Given that the opportunity to take on a Legal Ops sidekick had presented itself, Moon jumped at it. She invited Shilliam in as a guest lecturer, and their collaboration grew from there. Says Shilliam:

> Once we started teaching together, I could see the potential for true change. There is nothing better than teaching new attorneys, and we're looking mostly at two [lawyers], but sometimes three [lawyers] who are participating, and we are talking to them about all of the pieces and parts that might go into a Legal Operations practice and why those are important to students.

Moon and Shilliam have created a playground for ideas, discovery, and self-awareness against a backdrop that discourages all three. Anyone spot the anarchists within the citadel?

Law schools prepare students to be skeptics, to be cautious, to protect clients, to defend or attack as circumstances dictate. The lawyer is an encyclopedia of landmark cases and precedents, of the letter of the law, who dispenses advice upon demand. They are trained to operate within the legal silo, and to closely guard their legal knowledge, parsing it out only upon request, and at a price.

Collaboration outside the legal silo is not emphasized. Memory, research, and precedent trump thinking and collaborative problem-solving. If legal strategies are taught at all, they are rooted in the past. Innovation is tacitly discouraged.

Further, law students are encouraged to bend their personalities in order to fit into one of the accepted career tracks. In the extreme, vulnerability, empathy, even compassion must be controlled lest the budding lawyer be seen as weak or too "human."

Careerist, Opportunist, or Fatalist?

All these elements of the traditional law school education discourage students from sampling alternative career choices. The message is clear: You have three years to learn your trade so you can get going, pay off those student loans, and rise to the top. Any veering from the path could be both professionally and financially disastrous.

But personalities are a reality. By forcing all law students early on in their education into a few career options, law schools ignore the person behind the student. This dogmatic system leads to the production of too many square pegs jammed into round holes, and has disastrous long-term outcomes both for these lawyers and their clients.

In *The Generalist Counsel*, an earlier book co-authored by Prashant Dubey and Eva Kripilani, three types of groundbreaking legal professionals were identified: the Opportunist, the Careerist, and the Fatalist.[1] For Legal Ops professionals, we have added two overarching types: Creator and Responder.

Briefly, the Careerist is more planful and calculating (in a positive way). Advancement within the enterprise world is the Careerist's goal, and the sequence is more strategic. The Careerist will move into uncharted waters if the move makes sense from a career trajectory standpoint.

The Opportunist (an often pejorative term we have co-opted as something descriptive rather than negative) is driven to seek an evolving career and actively seizes opportunities that present themselves. The opportunities do not need to follow a logical sequence or lead to a specific landing spot. It is the experience the Opportunist desires.

The Fatalist essentially believes whatever opportunities come their way are inevitable and must be accepted. While still ambitious, the Fatalist would say they are guided by destiny. They do not actively seek to create opportunities for advancement. Thus, if they are destined to move into frigid uncharted waters, they will do so.

Students who go directly to law school with a four-year degree would benefit from an introduction to the Legal Ops career path so that they understand it is a viable option.

Careerist Seeks Direction

The Careerist may be entering law school with a specific career objective in mind—say, partner in a firm, or corporate counsel. By alerting them to the opportunities in Legal Ops as part of the standard curriculum, they may choose that career path once they have more information on it. The budding Opportunist may think, "Here's another path that may open up to me and it sounds exciting and remunerative and perhaps less cluttered." The Fatalist may sample a couple of courses and see it as their destiny.

1. Prashant Dubey and Eva Kripalani, *The Generalist Counsel: How Leading General Counsel Are Shaping Tomorrow's Companies* (New York: Oxford University Press, 2013), 16.

But here's where it gets more interesting. For those who do not go immediately to law school, but choose to go because they seek new (and perhaps specific) opportunities, a Legal Ops track could be attractive to all three. For instance, the Careerist is dissatisfied with their current track and seeks another road to a leadership position. They may be familiar with Legal Ops and seek a school that has a strong Legal Ops reputation.

Opportunist: My Mind Is Open

The Opportunist chooses to go to law school with an open mind, to see what options exist apart from what they have already experienced on the job. So many law school students are steered toward the law firm partnership path that round pegs in square holes are inevitable.

Connie Brenton, Vice President of Law, Technology, and Operations at NetApp, Inc., suffered for years as a litigator because it was the career path she chose almost randomly when she graduated from law school. No law school professor ever asked her to find out who she really was, and then consider what sort of law she might want to practice based on that self examination. Instead, as she describes in Chapter One, an acquaintance offered her an opportunity as a way out: to work on the business side at StorageTek. There, she serendipitously discovered her true calling, Legal Ops, by taking advantage of internal opportunities. If a law school offers coursework or a track to Legal Ops, it can make the school more attractive to this person—either during their first experience at law school, or as an older opportunistic lawyer seeking a new path.

Is It Fate or Good Fortune?

The Fatalist is another case altogether. This personality strongly believes in a personal destiny. They see patterns and signs that point to a certain path. The path may change as the fatalist makes their way almost hypnotically forward, guided by voices. There's a crucial difference between the Opportunist and the Fatalist. The former often chooses among an array of choices presented, while the latter is drawn inevitably toward one.

As a law student, the fatalist will be heavily influenced by a Svengali professor or by excelling in certain subjects—whether or not the fatalist has any special enthusiasm for the topic. If Legal Ops is not included in the core curriculum, the fatalist has no chance for a destiny along that path.

For the already employed fatalist lawyer, Legal Ops as destiny will be raised by choices at work championed by their bosses. Now, if the fatalist requires more academic training or credentialing to achieve their destiny, they would specifically seek out a law school such as Vanderbilt.

Caitlin Moon's human-centered design curriculum is already serving as a magnet for students searching for self-awareness as a guide to a career choice. Her innovative teaching style adds a depth to Vanderbilt's law program that is blossoming into a competitive advantage for the school.

> Students need a guided opportunity for self-awareness, and they can use that to plan their path forward. What is the role you are stepping into? Does it fit your persona? And for some students, it doesn't. It has often led a student to stop in that moment and redesign their path. There's a lot of power there for those who can tap into it.

Legal Ops in Academia

Lizzie Shilliam's path to Vanderbilt, and her serendipitous introduction to Caitlin Moon, marks her most emphatically as an Opportunist. As her career evolved, she found herself drawn to academia. A friend was consulting with the general counsel at Vanderbilt University in Nashville, and brought her in on the project. It was Lizzie's aha moment.

> I cannot tell you how different it is to work at an educational institution versus looking at the bottom line every quarter, because we don't have quarters that we have to make any certain dollar amount appear. We can really just focus on best practices and how we do things better all the time. And it is a really wonderful place to think about how the legal team can provide the best service to the university, to each department, to each Vice Chancellor, and to support the chancellor initiatives as well. So it's a wonderful place to be today.

Shilliam carved out a path to her dream job thanks to her early discovery of Legal Operations, and her willingness to dive into it. Consider her world: She implements Legal Operations for the entire university at her "day job," then jogs across campus to join Cat Moon in her human-centered design playground. Together, by broadening student horizons, they are determined to shake up the legal profession before it collapses under its own weight.

Moon's perspective is far wider than her students. She envisions positive change flowing from those hallowed halls of learning as her devotees launch themselves into the corporate world.

> As everyone should know by now, we face a lot of substantial challenges in our profession. My focus is on how we can bring the tools, methods, processes, and mindsets of innovation to meaningfully solving those challenges.

Shilliam has now witnessed firsthand the power of having an ambassador for Legal Ops in the position to influence young minds.

> The students really want to understand the business side. That's what Cat and I spend a lot of time thinking about: the business side, and how they might be just better attorneys by understanding what their clients need and what they want. That will make them a better attorney and [someone who provides] better customer service to those clients. It's a great program. Cat is

a driver of Legal Operations, sharing that information through many different avenues.

Legal Ops as Competitive Advantage

Today, Vanderbilt takes full advantage of the prestige Moon has brought to its legal studies program. It offers a range of coursework designed to lead to a Master of Legal Studies degree—both for lawyers and business professionals who are not lawyers. Here's how the school describes its program:

> Professionals in a wide range of industries must engage with legal questions as they navigate regulatory requirements while managing legal risk. Whether you work in compliance, human resources, technology, real estate, finance, or a variety of other fields, you'll discover value in acquiring a thorough understanding of the legal system.
>
> The online Master of Legal Studies (MLS) program from Vanderbilt Law School is for individuals who are not seeking to become lawyers, but rather who want specialized knowledge to solve law-related problems, identify areas of risk, and collaborate effectively with counsel. As organizations seek global business opportunities, gather an unprecedented volume of data, and outsource critical functions, it's vital for professionals to understand the legal implications of these decisions.[2]

A law school recruiting students who *won't* become lawyers? A law school professor asking students to engage in deep introspection before they choose a career? GenO is indeed rising, sometimes in the most unexpected places. And many of today's GenO leaders have never set foot in a law school classroom.

---

2. Vanderbilt Law School, "Online Master of Legal Studies," https://law.vanderbilt.edu/master-legal-studies/online-mls.

3

To Lawyer or Not to Lawyer—That Is the Question

A legal background certainly has some advantages. It helps in some ways, but it's far from being a necessary skill set to be successful with operations. There are so many skills that you need in this role that you're never going to come into it with all of them already. I think the more important skill set is a recognition around systematic thinking, and looking at ways to make things repeatable.

> MIKE HAVEN,
> *Head of Global Legal Operations,*
> *Intel Corporation*

When you are building a Legal Operations department, you immediately find yourself at a crossroads. Are you looking for lawyers who understand the flow of business, or business experts who are familiar with the law? How do you phrase the job description? Do they need to have a law degree? Can you say, "Law degree optional"? Or is an MBA preferred? Can you say, "Must have extensive revenue-producing experience" and find the person you want? When the résumés start to pour in, what are you screening for?

When this first quasi-legal, quasi-business role emerged, it was more a matter of casting about the law department for someone with a grasp of the new technologies hitting the market that claimed they could, for example, streamline eDiscovery processes. Or maybe someone in IT could handle it, with a little coaching from the lawyers. As these initial forays into Legal Ops began to prove worthy of further examination, writing the job description was perplexing. No wonder the Legal Ops pioneers relied on referrals to find the right people, and on their instincts about whether the candidate could manage this bifurcated task.

As Legal Ops has evolved, the job of building and then maintaining the department has eased somewhat. The pool of experienced candidates is larger. But the question lingers: Does the perfect fit need to have a law degree?

Perhaps requiring a law degree would be expedient. It makes the hiring decision more defensible. You don't have to explain to the higher-ups why you did *not* hire a lawyer. Problem is, you as the Legal Ops team builder know too much now. You understand that much of what a lawyer learns in law school, then in the law firm, must be unlearned if they are to excel in Legal Ops.

We posed this conundrum to our cadre of working Legal Ops professionals. We learned from our conversations that the ideal candidate must truly be a sort of renaissance person—one capable of identifying the essential elements of both law and business, and melding them into a vision of how work flows through the enterprise. It's OK if they went to law school. But a law degree isn't essential. By insisting on that diploma, you may well screen out the people best suited for the task.

Benefits of the Law Degree

Clearly, the law degree carries weight. It's an automatic ticket to the show. And the law degree does confer instant credibility when you're interacting with the law department. But does your candidate have what it takes to serve their internal clients in finance, sales, procurement, HR, marketing and IT? Protecting the company from risk is critical as a foundational principle. More important to the Legal Ops role is how well they perform in the day-to-day struggle to support lawyers in their negotiation of deals and turn transactions; to automate where possible the repetitive steps involved in contract management; to help with budgeting, planning and management reporting; and to create a smooth flow of work product across the enterprise.

Let's examine the benefits a law degree can confer on a Legal Ops candidate. We asked Bob Mignanelli, VP of Legal Strategy/Operations, Digital & Technology, & Procurement at Haleon, for his thoughts. Mignanelli earned his law degree from The Catholic University of America Columbus School of Law, but has chosen to put it to use in a Legal Operations capacity.

> Does a law degree help in certain scenarios? Sure, it does. I'll be very honest with you, it does, in a couple of different ways. Those credentials give me credibility with law departments. When I sit down and talk to lawyers, for the most part, I've probably done their job in some way, shape or form. I can understand where they're coming from. And then lawyers, we're an interesting group. We tend to gravitate towards our own a little faster than we gravitate towards folks who aren't lawyers. So that may give me a little bit more credibility, but again, it simply gets you through the door.
>
> But once you're at that table, once you're having those conversations, all the other skills are critical. And then when we think about setting strategy or executing on objectives to drive that strategy, all of the skills around project management and execution and organization, those all become critically important. The real challenge is bringing people together and to drive to a result. And as Legal Operations professionals, that's core to us. So the skills that I learned as a lawyer aren't the critical ones for being successful as a Legal Operations professional. So the legal experience, while a good context and background, then fades, while those other things become far more important to drive results.

Sally Guyer, Global Chief Executive Officer at World Commerce & Contracting, points out that law school graduates are entering the workforce steeped in legal defense theories. In certain roles, this serves them well. But once inside the corporation, the pressure is on to keep the legal documents moving along.

The contract law modules that we learn at law school are all about things that go wrong. It's all about case law. We're naturally conditioned as students to think about the things that go wrong and to assume that our role is to protect bad things from happening to our organization. And I'm not suggesting that that's not part of the role. Of course it is. But it misses the fundamental piece of being a business enabler, of enabling successful outcomes from the contracts that our business enters into. So if we want to be a strategic business partner, then we have to have a mindset shift, we have to shift from this preventive attitude to one of much greater optimism and how the legal team can participate in the delivery of successful outcomes.

Law: The Starting Point, Not the Endpoint

The lawyer who will succeed in a Legal Ops capacity must have the desire to do more than practice law. They will see themselves as directly contributing to the revenue side of the business through a revisionist view of business of law. Lawyers who have worked in a variety of roles understand that no monolithic legal document exists. Some do need to be reviewed line by line. Some do set the parameters for unique situations. But others are boilerplate, and, as such, can be reduced to the essentials of getting the deal done. They can be rapidly replicated, automated, created quickly from templates, amended on the fly. This is not how law schools train the typical student. But then most law schools are still focused on producing law firm partners rather than business enablers.

Lawyers who become business enablers tend to be self-made. Take Mike Haven, head of Global Legal Operations for Intel Corporation. A graduate of the University of the Pacific's McGeorge School of Law, Haven spent seven years with a law firm before jumping to NetApp in 2013 to run its Legal Operations function.

Haven describes himself as a "business-minded legal executive with substantial experience as inside and outside counsel." His background is incredibly diverse, spanning corporate Legal Operations, dispute resolution, investigations, intellectual property, privacy, securities, employment, and commercial transactions. He has served in some capacity in nearly every role where legal touches the business process at the enterprise level. At some point, Haven built himself a bridge to the business side. He has not crossed back.

> My point of view is that you don't have to be a lawyer to be a very good Legal Operations professional. It's a cross between a business role and a legal role. You may come at it from the business angle. You can come at it from the law angle. You can come at it from the IT angle. You can come at it from the finance angle, HR, procurement, and the list goes on.

> There are so many skills that you need in this role that you're never going to come into it with all of them already. You'll come in with a couple of the skills probably from those various angles. And you have to learn the rest on the job in a lot of cases. So, you have to come in with intellectual curiosity and a growth mindset, and be willing to always focus on learning. I am still learning every day. So, I think that's the key.

Lucy Bassli, founder and principal of InnoLaw Group, PLLC, calls these the Unicorn lawyers. Bassli cut her Legal Operations teeth at Microsoft prior to launching her own Legal Ops consulting business in 2018. Bassli was a practicing lawyer for many years.

> We're kind of a bit of a freak of nature, some of us. And I always say that with the greatest compliments when I spot someone and say, "You're another freak." We are not taught to think this way. We are taught to interpret the law. So we have to leverage skills that we have dormant and allow them to flourish. And you have to be in a place that allows them to flourish. So some of this just goes back to my own interests, my way of working, logical, analytical, not in the context necessarily of analysis of the law. Because yes, I was taught to do that, but that doesn't really help you navigate a contract management business process efficiently.

In the enterprise world, leaning too much on the law gums up the works, slows the pace of transactions, and robs them of their true value. It creates an adversarial relationship between legal and everyone else, a siloed organization where the two parties avoid talking to one another.

Result? The revenue-producing departments view legal as the pit where contracts go to die, where deals are killed, where money is spent but not produced. The lawyers assume a bunker mentality. They defend their turf, rarely venturing outside the department, and certainly not inviting "outsiders" in for a chat. They offer opinions on demand on their own timeline. And no one wins.

GenO Breaks Down Silos

As more lawyers have migrated to Legal Ops roles, the silos are weakening. Now, it is more common to encounter business enabling lawyers inside and outside the law department, contributing to strategic meetings, proposing innovative solutions, stripping away legal layering that added nothing to the transaction's outcome.

These unicorn lawyers have evolved skill sets representative of legal and business. Mike Haven ticks off the many areas of overlapping skills between successful practicing lawyers and Legal Ops staff.

> As a litigator, you've got to have thick skin, right? And as a Legal Operations pro, you've got to have thick skin. As a litigator, you have to be persuasive. As a Legal Operations pro, you have to be persuasive. As a litigator, you have to grind. You have to be resilient and patient, and keep grinding. And same with Legal Operations pros. So there's a lot of the skills, the inherent skills in litigation, that translated, I think for me, to Legal Operations. And also, just the fact that I was a partner in a big law firm helps with credibility, when I'm talking to our law firm partners or dealing with issues related to outside counsel. So, all of that has been helpful.

In the same breath, Haven cautions against placing too much emphasis on the degreed candidate.

> In terms of my view around the role of Legal Operations in the company, we are there to enable the business and guard the company. Enabling the business in the context of guarding the company, I guess, would be a good way to describe it.

So, if you're interviewing a candidate with a law degree, you want the unicorn, the rebel. The one who questions the model of the traditional lawyer: steady, solid, by-the-book, poking holes, creating a defense, but not offering creativity. The one who loves to bend the law just to see what might happen. What if, instead of saying, "No! That won't fly," I said, "Let's see if this will fly." Their résumés tend to reflect an eclectic taste for the law, perhaps a public defender post for starters, then a litigation firm, followed by a stint with a patent firm, then off to a corporate law department. These lawyers are looking for something beyond the routine application of a legal specialty. Legal Ops provides a natural bridge for a lawyer with a creative mind and a love of business.

Law-Smart—But Not a Lawyer

Increasingly, GenO managers are hiring people who are not trained in "lawyering," and do not possess a law degree. They are looking for tech-savvy candidates with deep business process experience who have demonstrated their ability to collaborate across departments. It's assumed that such a person knows the intersection of legal and business, they know how to manage that intersection to reduce turnaround times, and they are comfortable managing the risks of cycle reduction in the greater context of getting the deal done.

The first professionals without law degrees to populate Legal Ops had to have significant tech chops. This assumption of tech mastery was natural enough. The pressures to convert the enterprise's mountain of data and documents to a searchable electronic database to meet the demands of a discovery request sounded an alarm. Who can do this? The job quite logically landed at IT's doorstep. In the law department, it went to someone who understood technology and how its application could be used to lower cost, accelerate cycle times, and offer visibility into risk levers. This was often the first step toward creation of the Legal Operations professional in a law department.

But as the applications for technology to streamline the legal process expanded, the process for more fully exploiting the opportunities that arose took the task far beyond IT's capacity. Need arose for a new kind of "internal legal business process maven," steeped as well in workflow experience. This person would have to understand where technology could be applied to the legal process to breach the dams that were restraining workflow. Then, they would have to create and sell a solution internally.

This was no easy task. Often the solution was unbudgeted. Multiple departments had to buy in. Then there was the law department's aversion to change. Would this solution undermine our authority? Put inside counsel out of business? Disrupt our relationship with outside counsel? Will we have to meet with sales and marketing types?

Limits of Lawyering

The skills needed to unlock the revenue-enhancing promises of legal tech were considerable. And perhaps least among them was a law school degree.

Steph Corey, CEO and co-founder of UpLevel Ops, and who does not have a law degree, is a strong advocate for staffing up Legal Ops with professionals who are not lawyers. She would prefer to work with someone who has mastered the operational side, who is process- and transaction-driven, who understands the role that legal plays in getting deals done.

To build a solid Legal Ops team, the leader's right-hand person should be first and foremost someone who has good chemistry, somebody who's always looking for a better way of doing things. And that might be a hard skill to suss out just as you're looking at résumés. The law degree may not be what you're looking for. Law school is based on precedent and what happened in the 1800s. Business schools just like to be as efficient as possible—and efficiency is never even mentioned in law school. So I think for this role, you most certainly don't need to be a practicing lawyer. As an ops manager, you don't have to think of the legal strategy of how to do that, but you have to understand what the legal strategy is going to be to do that or push the lawyers in that direction.

I mean, there were times I wished I had a law degree, simply due to the fact that I would've been held in higher regard. But that's a stupid reason to go to school for something. And it's not that the knowledge or the degree itself would've helped me anyway. It's just that I can't tell you how many times early in my career, literally there was one person on the GC staff who pushed to not have me in meetings because they thought privilege would be broken, really stupid things. And thank goodness the GCs I always worked for were like, "No, she's staying. She's the one who's going to make sure we get this stuff done, actually." So it was a foolish argument.

One side note from Corey: Not having a law degree often proved useful when dealing with the corporate lawyers.

At first I had to fight for a seat at the table because I wasn't a lawyer. Once I got there, not being a lawyer actually was more beneficial to developing relationships among the GC staff. Because I was not a lawyer, I was not a threat to the lawyers in any way. I was never going to take their job.

Notching the Early Win

I think our sources are in agreement that an ideal blended team would include law degrees, MBAs, tech credentials, and considerable cross-departmental operations experience. But there's nothing like an early win to prove to your internal customers that you have enough understanding of the law as it applies to business to get the job done. Steve Harmon, COO and General Counsel of law company Elevate, describes just such a case.

> One of the key things that we identified early on was that the legal department was perceived as slowing business down; I think that's a common perception. As such, we set out a goal to reduce the cycle time of contract negotiation, for both our inbound contracts and our outbound sales contracts.
>
> I won't represent that it was an easy process, but we methodically approached the problem of, how do we optimize our internal contract negotiations? How do we routinize that, in a way that we can reduce total cycle time? And so, over a multi-year period, we were able to reduce cycle time for sales contracts from fourteen days to nine days, as an example.
>
> Now, that was a big shift, but from a top-line perspective, it made us very popular with the sales team, to reduce the amount of time that was required and the number of cycles required to negotiate those contracts. But it also had a real financial benefit. The sooner your customer can start placing orders, the sooner your organization can start recognizing revenue on those contracts.
>
> And at an organization the size of Cisco, when I left, Cisco was a $50 billion revenue company. That's a billion dollars a week in revenue, $200 million every business day. If you start to calculate just the float on reducing cycle times by collecting revenue five days faster, that's a material benefit to the organization.
>
> The operational focus on shortening the timeline to getting the deal done, realizing the revenue, and maximizing the profit will quickly dispel any concerns about the academic credentials of those responsible for streamlining the process.

A Legal Ops professional talking about float—the time delta between book balance and available balance and the ability to earn interest in that window—that is most certainly a businessperson who "happens" to be a lawyer/Legal Ops professional. Now, Steve Harmon may be viewed by some readers as unique in his ability to describe and manage these scenarios—but is he? The point of this book is that many professionals are shaping themselves as professionals in a manner that Steve did. It's notable that on his way to the pinnacle of the profession, he constantly reached across and down and pulled others along and up. More on this later, but we feel this (pay it forward) dynamic is a core attribute of the Legal Ops community that is a leading indicator of our unlimited potential.

Here's the task: As a GenO team builder, you have to look beyond the degree and the résumé. You're looking for a good listener, a robust communicator, an efficiency expert. The curious yet analytic mind that can track a process from one end to the other to find the snags and snarls. Someone with just enough legal and tech knowledge to be dangerous, but who can also sell the solution to the CFO, the GC, and even the CEO.

GenO Rising

Harmon brings our discussion back to the initial question: Do you have to have a law degree to excel in Legal Ops?

The big focus of Legal Operations, in my estimation, is to develop your processes in a way that you can offer predictable outcomes. And those predictable outcomes are very valuable to the organization. They're very valuable to the lawyers that you are supporting, as well as to your other internal customers. Given the choice between taking a new lawyer directly out of law school or taking someone with a strong project management background, or a Six Sigma background, I would almost always take the strong project manager.

Whether a lawyer or not, these professionals are using a Legal Ops mindset to go outside the boundaries of the law department. They are becoming strategic business enablers, rising from the depths of being mavens of law department efficiency to drive business value throughout the company. This is the Rise of Legal Operations — GenO, we welcome you ...

4

Technocrat or Process Maven?

Gain perspective on what is in it for the people that are actually going to be utilizing the solution. if you don't keep that in mind, you're going to build something that they're going to just want to go around, they're going to avoid it. They're going to not use it. And that solves nothing.

GERALD WRIGHT, *former leader of the Global Contract Solutions Group, Intel Corporation, retired*

Legal technology in the workplace is growing at an impressive pace. Having legal and operational minds that are trained in this domain and who understand the business implications creates a great pool of talent for the entire enterprise to draw upon. At the same time, one does not need to have a law degree, or a STEM degree, to excel. The person who will master this role understands the flow of business across the enterprise and where legal needs arise in the course of that flow.

For the most part, corporate legal documents do not originate in the legal department. They may be created there, but only after a request comes in from elsewhere: marketing, sales, human resources, procurement. A copy of the document may reside in legal as a matter of record (usually on a rarely accessed, dusty digital shelf). But those who will actually be working with, and from, the document as they conduct their business need to have a copy closer to home. When someone asks, "Well, what does the nondisclosure agreement say?" retrieval must be in real time—not through a process that takes the team outside the department in search of the language.

It is in this space that the Legal Ops team can prove its value.

Through their mastery of technology, and their understanding of how it applies to the intersection of law and business, they can make the magic happen. The law in today's enterprise depends upon technological support to achieve its ends, because the need to know what the document stipulates is immediate. The making of (or preventing the loss of) money cannot wait while someone in the legal department searches for the contract, reviews it, crafts an opinion, and finally sends it along.

Instead, the GenO magician says, "Here's the NDA. I've had it reviewed (translation: likely with a combination of technology and people) based on what you said you needed to know, and here's our course of action. Oh, and we should notify legal that the vendor did indeed violate it so we can void it before any more damage is done."

Think of legal technology as corporate mycelia, weaving throughout the enterprise, providing the connective tissue that keeps business humming along. It makes its appearance at the intersections of departments—law and every other department: sales and accounting; procurement and finance; IT and HR. Where a need arises to review a matter of law or create a legal document, Legal Ops is there to ensure it gets done quickly, efficiently, and correctly.

Our GenO interviewees have, over time, rounded out their skill sets so that they bring big-picture visioning to the role. But most of the early GenO converts came to the job with one of two perspectives: either through a technical lens, or a process lens.

Leading with Technology

Gerald Wright, retired leader of the Global Contract Solutions Group at Intel Corporation, shaped the Legal Operations juggernaut there for more than two decades. When he came to Intel, he brought plenty of experience working with lawyers. However, his early speciality was figuring out how to apply technology to the management of intellectual property. In a real sense, he was a self-taught tech maven.

Wright earned his intellectual property bones at a midsize firm in Portland, Oregon, in the 1990s, learning about trademarks, patents, and copyright. These are the legal pillars that support an IP-driven corporation's ultimate objective: to sell products and services. In order for the profit-making side to achieve its full potential, legal had to keep pace. Wright's technical background allowed him to envision how technology, applied to law within the enterprise, moved the entire organization forward rather than holding it back.

But Wright was so early to the game that he had to create his own technological tools to build systems for managing intellectual property. This experience—a painstaking process, he admits—provided him, and his internal clients, with a foundation for organizing legal documents so they could be efficiently tracked, retrieved, and shared when needed. This was a major leap forward for a budding Legal Ops professional. It's a business process facilitation of a different level, and it raises sometimes uncomfortable questions. What do I need to understand in order to enable lawyers with technology that facilitates their process? How do you build relationships with those individuals so that you could facilitate their work through a technology that you built? Also, this was a law firm, not a corporation, and most law firms have internal silos built around individual partners and their book of business and clients.

When Wright moved on to Intel's law department as an IP specialist, he faced challenges. The legal and business sides weren't collaborating smoothly. Technological gaps existed that were holding up the process. Though it may be a stereotype, IP lawyers are incredibly smart on a technical level. In order to support their pursuits, it was crucial to get them to think beyond the technical elements of what they were doing, and facilitate their process.

Wright needed to convince the lawyers that his technical solutions would not only support their work, but would enhance their esteem among the business units. Protecting the intellectual property of one's employer is a serious task. Leadership assumes it's being closely guarded. The breaches—not the day in, day out protection—are what gets the C-suite's attention. So the IP lawyer is cautious by nature, and trusts the process that has worked so far.

Wright says it's essential to understand this lawyerly mindset. Consider this challenge he accepted: The business side is clamoring for a more efficient, faster-to-revenue process, and they see IP lawyers as the snag. The lawyers say the review process does not lend itself to shortcuts. How to satisfy both customers? At Intel, he says, he was fortunate to work with lawyers who were hungry for the solutions he was crafting.

> Working with the lawyers day-to-day, you learn their trade. It's about understanding your audience and their needs, and being able to articulate it in some way in a solution that makes sense to them at the center. You have to understand what their pain is, and articulate what the benefit is to them before you propose a solution that may be technology-enabled. What's in it for my audience? Ultimately, how do they have more efficiency in executing their roles? We're providing automation that solves problems for all the business units.

> But if the process begins with IP, you need to be sensitive to the culture. Gain perspective on what is in it for the people that are actually going to be utilizing the solution. if you don't keep that in mind, you're going to build something that they're going to just want to go around, they're going to avoid it. They're going to not use it. And that solves nothing.

Learn What You Need to Know

Steph Corey, CEO and co-founder of UpLevel Ops, offers a case study of someone whose understanding of the requirements of the business process led her to a Legal Ops role. In other words, the process maven. What does a process maven do? Many things comprise this role. But in a sentence, one might say the process maven is the creator and enforcer of the systems and structures that keep the company moving. The process maven presents a legal mindset to business solutions, but also brings a business-objective lens to the legal aspects that arise during the course of business.

Corey has multiple academic credentials: She has her undergraduate degree in economics, and an MBA in business administration and economics from Lehigh University's College of Business. In 1999, she was responsible for creating and managing cash management systems for a financial services firm when an opportunity to join the then-exclusive GenO club presented itself.

Hewlett-Packard wanted to create a Legal Operations team to better manage legal costs in general and outside counsel fees in particular. Corey's operations skills, her finance expertise, and her process mastery looked good on paper—even without a law degree or advanced tech knowledge. She lived in the documents flow and knew where to look for the disruptions in the flow.

> HP was looking for somebody who could come in and get them organized and manage the finances. They did have a tech team in place. And I thought, "I can learn the tech piece of this, and I've already got the finance experience, so let's do this." I made those IT folks my besties because I needed their help and I needed their resources. I was in my early twenties and they trusted me to give me this big role, and I figured I would just do this for a year or so and head into one of the businesses. I'm not a lawyer, why would I ever stay in the legal department? And here we are twenty-plus years later, still doing it.

Corey says HP was the perfect place for a process maven's introduction to Legal Ops.

> They literally called the role Legal Operations. They knew what they were looking for. They knew they wanted somebody in there who can bring some structure to these 200 attorneys and paralegals and other types of legal professionals. I think it was the first probably officially designated Legal Operations role in all of California, certainly in Silicon Valley, but probably all of California.

GenO as Business Enabler

The explosion of corporate litigation and the simultaneous trend to codify more of the day-to-day corporate activities in contracts overwhelmed the traditional legal document management system and processes. New technologies emerged to manage both the volume and the demand for immediate access to such documents. But few within the enterprise understood how these technologies could be harnessed.

That's when the GenO cadre really began to develop. Staff lawyers seeking new opportunities outside the legal department spotted an internal growth opportunity. Tech mavens in IT who were looking to expand their knowledge and turf were drawn to Legal Ops. Middle managers who understood the need for new strategies to store and retrieve documents critical to the business flow joined the GenO ranks. Contract management as an initiative, initially owned and managed by the law department, thrust Legal Ops into the role of strategic business enabler.

As a result of the rise in stature of GenO, legal technology is rapidly becoming enterprise business technology. Emerging technological solutions support the process maven's dedication to enhancing document flow. Meanwhile, the tech mavens on the team understand where the process can benefit from their expertise, and are constantly seeking out and vetting better ways to marry tech and process. Working in concert, they truly support the entire enterprise in its quest to streamline the flow of legal documents.

This dynamic drove these professionals to focus on their business acumen and business process knowledge, and challenged them to consider how technology could be used as an enabler. Should the law department take the lead? Or should they be brought along? Did the emerging technology mean legal could be freed of thousands of repetitive actions to focus more on the broader legal landscape? Asking such questions became the key animating call to action for Legal Ops to become strategic business enablers.

These tech-minded specialists exist and are thriving. A new generation of Legal Operations professionals is going way past the boundaries of the law department, emerging as strategic business enablers. Their ability to discern between the benefits of technology and the benefits of "lawyerly" thinking drives their contributions to the whole. This can be expanded upon to mean process-oriented thinking, one that operates more by the book—a book still being written.

GenO operates at a place where the set objectives are enabled by strategies that allow one to achieve their desired outcome. The connection between the outcome and the strategic objectives is something that a strategic business enabler needs to have. This way of thinking certainly highlights the business-first mindset, one that is so crucial for becoming a strategic business enabler. No stakeholder will care that a Legal Ops professional took a business mindset if the outcomes are achieved.

Oftentimes, this means finding a business problem and proactively trying to solve it. In many cases, there will be roadblocks. The true process maven views roadblocks as challenges and learning opportunities. If the roadblock is technological, the process maven knows where to look for a solution. If legal, they draw upon their legal knowledge. If it is cultural, they will use it to test and sharpen their soft skills.

But solutions cost money, and having foresight to budget correctly for technology is an essential skill that must be mastered by the successful GenO leader. The challenge when establishing a Legal Ops presence is to negotiate a reasonable budget with those who control the corporate pursestrings.

The Power of the Budget

New technology is always intimidating. Without precedents for comparison, the cost of the software and hardware required can be daunting. In the new SaaS (software as a service) environment, where bespoke pricing models abound, companies are still trying to understand all the costs of technology. Yet new technology, the tech and process mavens both know, is what will drive the cost savings (and eventual revenue generation) associated with Legal Ops. Legal Ops must win the support of the leadership team in order for appropriate budgeting to happen in advance. When establishing an independent Legal Operations function, having an appropriate budget is critical for the successful launch. But even a legacy Legal Ops department must be prepared to make its case annually, given the very nature of the role: to identify new tools that will support the ongoing streamlining of the flow of legal documents and increase legal department and enterprise efficiency, while minimizing risk.

Thus our GenO leaders must make a strong return-on-investment (ROI) case with the CFO in language the CFO understands. With support from a visionary CFO or General Counsel—one who sees the need for the investment, understands the return on that investment, and builds it into the budget—Legal Ops can do its magic.

Tom Sabatino, Executive Vice President and Chief Legal Officer at Rite Aid, was among those who pioneered the Legal Ops profession. His early insights into the power that was unleashed when legal and business minds conjoined, influenced a generation of internal changemakers. In the early days, though, there was little precedent for the scope of work he envisioned. Fortunately, Sabatino had colleagues who shared his vision.

> The supportive CFO understands what we bring, and we understand what the CFO brings. So there's a sort of natural synergy there, and we tend to operate closely together. What I have found is you actually can go to a CFO and say to him or her, "Hey, look. We've got a system we want to put in place here that's going to expedite contracts. We're going to be able to get these contracts faster, we're going to be able to recognize revenue more quickly; we're going to take stuff out of the system that sort of gunks up the works." They'll say, "OK, where do I write the check?" Which is a great thing to have your CFO tell you, as they're going to see that in action.
>
> When you bring those two things together in an effective way, the CFO's happy, the lawyers are happy, business transactions are expedited, and things are going faster and faster. It creates a virtuous cycle for the organization. Then you are able to continue to lift the game for everybody involved. It's a critical component of what we do.

Bringing the Budget to Life—Getting Funded

Establishing that budget requires the savvy Legal Ops pro to call on an array of skills when setting the tone for the work ahead. They need to know the technological landscape—in other words, what is currently available to do the job? Then they have to determine what problems need to be solved, and what they will likely cost. Does the culture support technological solutions? Then, what is the tolerance for spending? What can be achieved with different levels of investment? Is it CapEx (capital expenditure) or OpEx (operating expense)—and know the difference. Often knowing *how* to get funded is different than rationalizing the funding. GenO professionals understand the difference between a balance sheet and a P&L (profit and loss) statement. And then, they have to sell their solution to those who control the purse strings.

Tommie Tavares-Ferreira, Senior Corporate and Commercial Counsel for healthcare payment platform provider Cedar Cares, Inc., runs Legal Operations for the company. When she assumed the post in December of 2022, her first move was to find out what the General Counsel had in mind to fund the work.

> I wanted to find out what they were willing to put behind me being able to get the job done that they expected me to get done. I think one of my first few questions was, not how much specifically will you commit, but do you have a certain percentage of your budget earmarked for technology? So asking, "What's your stake in this?"
>
> So really in the early days, I built the roadmap for the first year. Probably four months of it was a learning and listening tour. It was going around the whole business. It was socializing with people, meeting with heads of departments, and deputies, and people that might be my biggest stakeholders and learning, "What are the pain points? What are you trying to achieve here? How do I get the legal and compliance expertise out of our department and to you in the best way?"

Every budget needs to be grounded in business objectives ... and, yes ... as outlined above, outcomes. The GenO professional needs to do the listening tour to understand the business objectives but then they need to identify budgetary spend that is mapped to outcomes.

Beware the Previous Playbook

Several of our GenO pros cautioned against depending too heavily on the playbook that worked in the last gig. Those who live by the playbook may also die by it if they don't do their homework.

Once she had a sense of what the needs were across departments, Tavares-Ferreira could broach the budget subject with leadership from a stronger position. She says there's always the temptation when one changes employers to simply bring budgeting assumptions from the previous position to the new one. But that's a mistake. Better to start fresh.

> Even if you do have a playbook from the past, you do want to approach the new company without a lot of assumptions. You want to approach it from that very business-centric sense of, "How am I solving your specific problems? Not the job I had last time, and the money I had last time, and the tooling I had, but how am I solving your specific problems?"

> When you lay out a decision that needs to be made in such a way that someone makes the decision you're hoping they make, because you've laid out a pretty viable argument—you've done your research and you've done your homework—and they get to the same place that you get to, and they've made that decision, I think that that's a win-win.

Tom Sabatino cautions that, when doing your due diligence on the new job, should you find gaping holes in the process, you may face an uphill battle to get the money you need to do the job. This may be a sign of a corporation that has not bought into the value proposition of Legal Ops. The leadership team may not even be aware of what that attitude is costing the company. Toss the old playbook out the window at this point.

> I will tell you when it doesn't work, when you don't have the right systems in place, the amount of friction that it causes in the organization and the amount of lost opportunity and lost revenue is probably something people don't focus a lot on. I've come to companies where we didn't have good systems. When that exists, you encounter a huge amount of effort and time on everyone's part—from the lawyers, to the finance people, to the business people, the sales people—to achieve far less. It slows the organization down in a way that's not helpful. So that's really, to me, the downside risk you have when you don't spend the money, spend the effort, spend the opportunity cost to get this thing moving. Understanding the reality of a situation is the foundation for understanding how to change it.

Making the Big Shift

When the knowledge of technology combines with the logic and structure of a process-oriented thinker, big shifts begin. While it doesn't necessarily mean one needs to "be technical," it does imply that one understands the capabilities and limitations of technology and how to apply technology to achieve outcomes in a more efficient manner.

Thus we find GenO individuals who have sharpened skills in not only the practical, business side of legal, but also the tech side—even if those skills must be learned on at least a functional level. An effective Legal Ops professional must be able to pull from elements of the technocrat, as well as the process maven. It is crucial to the GenO movement to demonstrate the importance of being a process-oriented thinker, as well as having the ability to understand the importance and possible implementations of technology. Technology was once simply a tool for legal actions to be executed. Today, technology has become the catalyst of the legal process that lies within a larger enterprise business process.

GenO professionals understand technology is not the elixir, it's an enabler. The approach must be very business-centric, but also human-centric. How am I solving *your* specific problems? Legal Ops is getting expert at the soft skill of listening, of hearing what people actually need and what they don't need, before making a recommendation that they, and everyone else, will have to live with. Some departments may have a higher degree of tech aversion than others. That's where GenO needs to reassure them that they do not have to understand the intricacies of the solution to benefit from it. If you don't internalize the human centricity of it—that there are actually human beings involved in the process—things start to fall apart.

Donovan Bell, Director of Information and Contract Experience (Global Legal Operations) for Intel Corporation, as well as a council member of the Corporate Legal Operations Consortium, advises Legal Ops to be vigilant about the opportunities presented by the fact that contracting is fundamentally a human-centric business process. Consequently, the humans involved in the flow and lifecycle of contract documents leads to inefficiencies in the work process.

> The goal is to reach a point of automation for some of your low-risk areas. You truly make it to where you can drive more [contract] templates, and leverage these templates to help streamline the process so we now don't need such a substantial legal review or legal involvement. You want to establish places where you can streamline the workflow with automation, where you have an approval workflow or process in place so you don't need the ongoing review. You've typically taken either another system or a manual process offline, one that might be even pretty pristine, but the cycle time of it is slowing you down. You need to streamline it. What's causing the snag? People or process? Oftentimes, because of the people's involvement, you end up having to dig into that more frequently.

> So you use your systems and your tools to hopefully automate, streamline, simplify. From a workflow automation perspective, it's much simpler, much more streamlined. So finding those small, low-hanging fruit pieces is what I look for. That's what wins people over to your way of thinking: You show them immediate benefits without a huge investment on their part.

Gerald Wright's study of the legal-to-business process at Intel revealed that both parties had room for improvement.

> Sometimes the legal review process was slow because the work they were receiving caused an extended legal review process. We enabled the business folks with key knowledge about what the lawyers were looking for when they're reviewing their content. They took this training and knowledge, and it helped them be more efficient. They were hungry for this information because they didn't want Legal to be a roadblock for them. This gave them an opportunity to become knowledgeable about

Legal needs for information, in the process accelerating the cycle time for Legal needs.

Any Legal Operations professional should internalize the fact that at some point, any legal business process that's being executed has a connection with the business and has a business outcome. You directly insert yourself in the workflow with the attorneys that are doing deals, and you're supporting them in terms of executing the deal. You get right into the heart of the business. There were times where I would sit on the staff of a GM and be the surrogate legal rep in the room for the attorney. Looking back, we've driven so much efficiency, it takes probably five to ten minutes to get an NDA signed now. When I started, it was ten to fifteen days.

Tom Sabatino explains that the ideal GenO pro must be able to trace the flow of legal work through departments to ensure that the process is truly as efficient as it's been advertised. Oftentimes, he has found, there are snags throughout that no one had put together previously. Snags that, when identified, were costing the company plenty of dough in lost time.

At Schering-Plough, the law department was getting dinged for slowing the procurement process down around IT contracts, computer contracts, and all that kind of stuff. I had responsibility for procurement in addition to the legal function [at many companies]. I could get everyone together and say, "How are we going to make this better? Where are the sticking points? Where are the things that don't work?" So it was never just about drafting a contract, it's about understanding the process of how things happen.

"It's always getting stuck in the law department" was sort of the thing we got. So we finally said, "OK, let's find out if that's true and how we can make this thing go faster." We ultimately ended up putting in a contract management system that actually expedited us. But we went to basic principles like, "OK, let's measure how long it takes to get stuff done and where the true bottlenecks exist and why." It was not a blame-finding exercise—it was a forensic exercise that was truly collaborative at its core. The metrics helped lead us to the solution, and facilitated buy-in by the parties.

In such cases, the process maven has the credibility to identify where time and money are being lost, and the tech maven is ready with the solution. This combined expertise is what sets Legal Ops apart, and what builds its internal reputation as expediter.

Integrating Perspectives

Oftentimes the perspective shifts with the introduction of technology. It's not really a technology implementation as much as it is rolling out a business process that happens to be enabled by technology. When GenO is having conversations with their business colleagues, they're not talking about the mouse-clicks here and there. In some cases they're saying, "Let me tell you what the functionality of the technology is and how it'll help you."

A good technocrat also understands the benefit of a community and the multiple perspectives their community shares with them. Technology is changing so quickly and improving so quickly, it's very important to create a community so that you can pick up the phone and say, "Have you tried it? What went wrong? What do I need to look out for? And where's the low-hanging fruit?"

When we deploy technology, we need to ensure that we're getting all of the stakeholder views. So when we want to drive efficiency, we cannot do it alone. We cannot do it in one department without thinking about the consequences to others. GenO professionals make sure they are embracing their business partners around the organization and talking about what the right solutions are.

Be Transparent About the Learning Curve

A note of caution: Strategic technocrats are aware that newly implemented technology will not work perfectly right out of the gate. They accept that. It is imperative to let everybody know that new technology evolves in phases, that it is responsive rather than reactive. Feedback on its performance will be integrated by Legal Ops and IT quickly, so let them know how it's working. As an early adopter, your technology provider becomes a real partner and they can redesign or create solutions specifically for you.

Ideally, Legal Ops can tolerate making mistakes and tweaking in real time. Embrace technology and don't be afraid to experiment and understand that it's not going to be perfect out of the gate. It's an iterative process, and the way technology is used at every juncture is very different. The power of a GenO Legal Operations professional is the fact that you understand that your process should be used as a vehicle for you to understand if and how those technologies apply to you. Stepping back and identifying pain points in your process is key to understanding the potential for technological implementation.

In closing, our thoughts on marrying technical and process expertise to achieve a seamless workflow, we want to circle back to the human element. All the technological bells and whistles in the world won't drive efficiency and, ultimately, profitability, unless the people who work with you buy into it. The history of the technological era is littered with the rusting remnants of perfectly good solutions that failed to integrate people into the programming.

Thus a huge piece of the Legal Ops challenge lies in the seamless interface between machine and human. It has become fashionable to push user interface testing to the very end of the line. In fact, eliminating user experience altogether happens far too often in the rush to meet deadlines. "Let crowdsourcing handle

UX," is the justification. The customer is always right, and sometimes, rather than complaining, they simply walk away.

Our tech maven Gerald Wright has a few thoughts on that topic:

> It's just so critical to take the time to focus on that user experience. And I'm no user experience UX/UI expert, but I do try to apply the golden rule as much as I can, with some modification. "Do unto others what you want done to yourself." I don't want to see a screen of content that makes no sense to me. I just need to click one button and I'm done. But instead, there's all this other stuff on the screen that I have to solve. If I don't want to see it, I don't think others will want to see it, so I'm not going to subject them to it.
>
> So yeah, our job in operations in the contracting space can be quite tedious sometimes. But it's important work because ultimately it's going to save tons of cycle times, and we're going to get contracts done faster. And when you get contracts done faster, that means you get paid faster. So if your customer buys into it, it ultimately hits the bottom line. Don't make it difficult to buy into. Remember, you are working with humans. Factor that in.

It's a matter of corporate interdepartmental bridge-building, engineered and architected by an evolving and ever more essential breed of GenO. One area of focus, especially when establishing the role of Legal Ops, must be metrics. Your long-term objective, of course, is to demonstrate the ongoing contributions your team can make. But in today's corporation, new ventures can take root more quickly if they set specific metric goals and achieve—or exceed—them. This will be the topic of our next chapter.

5

Metrics, Measurements, and Management Controls

For those that really want to be competitive moving forward, efficiency and making sure you get your return on investment is big. If I'm going to give you this dollar, tell me what you're going to do with it and tell me why it's a good thing to do. The more metrics, the more control you have over that flow, the better off you are.

CARRICK CRAIG, *Senior Counsel, Miller Canfield*

There cannot be enough emphasis on the importance of GenO leaders understanding and incorporating metrics into their craft. This, combined with an understanding of risk and controls, allows for Legal Ops to be the primary trendsetter in the business. Metrics can be used to achieve success on initiatives, get executive support, funding, and also further one's career. In today's enterprise, metrics can unlock the potential that GenO'ers know exists in their wizardry. It is the proof of their practice.

Effective Legal Ops specialists know the value of obtaining and analyzing key measurements and metrics of processes in and around the business. Time and money are the biggest indicators of success and efficiency in a company. They are coded in the language of the business, metrics, and data. Every high-functioning business would benefit from a deeper understanding of their processes. Not only does a grasp of metrics improve the efficiency of the Legal Ops department, it can be further established within the culture of the entire business.

If one finds themselves in a new role where executives are saying, "I want you to do X, Y, or Z," have the confidence as a professional to say, "What we first have to do is understand where we are, before we start the journey to where you want us to get to." This means establishing a foundation of metrics and understanding what the challenges are in the Legal Ops department and business as a whole.

Slow Down to Speed Up

At the intersection of the business and the legal world, there is constant pressure to accelerate. As a strategic business enabler, sometimes, it's okay to guide folks and say, "Slow down. We first have to document our baseline or our foundation." That's a critical lesson for people to internalize, especially some of the younger GenO professionals who are entering the industry. They must remember to have the confidence to say that, to emphasize the desirability of stepping back and assessing prior to taking action.

A lot of times, there is pushback from the pre-established way of doing things. Collecting data and metrics, and subsequently analyzing them to be implemented for beneficial measures, takes additional time and energy that extends outside of the "typical" workday. While there may be initial hesitancy to collect these metrics, the benefits in terms of time saved and money saved over the long term far outweigh the initial investment of time and effort.

Where to Start?

Asking fundamental questions is the key to understanding what works smoothly and what can be improved upon. How much have we actually budgeted for this enterprise? What can we get done with the economic parameters that you've set? Which metrics are meaningful to the internal clients we serve?

Steve Harmon is Chief Operating Officer and General Counsel of Elevate. His experience in understanding and communicating the value of metrics allowed him to save his department and company time and energy. The motivation to create an efficient system within the company is quintessential for GenO professionals' maintenance of level of excellence in their daily work processes.

> Early in my Legal Operations career, we did a time-and-motion study of the work being done by our contract negotiators, our sales-facing lawyers, and professionals. In that study, we identified 14% of their time was allocated to administrative tasks. Of that 14%, 11% was dedicated to administrative tasks directly related to our contract management system—managing contracts and pushing them through the system. By doing that study, and taking that data to our timekeepers and contract negotiators, we facilitated a very welcomed conversation. "We can give you 11% of your time back to focus on higher-margin, higher-worth activities." If we had just come in and said, "We'd like to come in and take tasks off your plate, and reduce the number of contract negotiators we need," the response would've been very different than the response we received. You really have to focus on that org adoption piece.

Harmon strategically chose a study that would produce clear outcomes. His experience and intuition told him, "This is an area that needs to be examined and improved." With the metrics in hand, he was then able to demonstrate in terms that his internal clients understood the benefits of breaking down a process and laying bare the low-hanging fruit in the contract management system. Score one modest win for Legal Ops, but a much larger step forward for GenO'ers.

'Quick Wins,' Nuanced Pace

How do you measure productivity? How do you validate utilizing Legal Ops services inhouse? Studies, surveys, and analyzing data are three ways in which Legal Ops can create opportunities for increased efficiency within a company.

There is certainly a bit of finesse required to implementing these key data into your process. A GenO professional who goes full force on collecting and analyzing data and metrics may miss the more nuanced elements of Legal Ops that make up our soft skills. Browbeating people with numbers to get them to do what you want may give one a brief advantage. But it builds resentment and lack of trust. A balance between the human side of metrics and the data side of metrics opens the doors for implementations that satisfy not only the numerical benefits of data and metric, but also the human side.

Having a high EQ (better known as emotional intelligence) will pair nicely with effective metric curation and analysis. High EQ allows for understanding human dynamics, the basis in which metrics and measurements can be understood. This emotional intelligence, combined with an understanding of how to collect and implement metrics and measurements, allows a Legal Ops professional to bring it all together in order to make for a successful journey.

Applying EQ to Metrics

Tom Sabatino, Executive Vice President and Chief Legal Officer at Rite Aid, explains the value of soft skills when implementing metrics and measurements into a game plan for further implementation.

> There is not just the quantitative metrics around how fast a contract goes through the system, but really having a high EQ around relationship-building. We've seen a lot of tension between the chief procurement officer and the General Counsel where the procurement organization are trying to be strategic category managers, for example, and they view the legal organization as a deal prevention department. When we send it over for legal review, all of a sudden you're talking about data protection provisions, or is there PII [personally identifiable information]? Or what are the insurance levels that

are needed? And we're adding all this time to it, and all of a sudden the business requester of a contract from procurement is saying, "Why is it taking so long?" And we've found that the General Counsel and their organization can actually codify some of their legal desires within things like contract templates.

They can say, "Let me actually bless a contract template that contains language that I'm comfortable with and empower you, procurement organization, to use fallback provisions and negotiate this on your own. And we'll give you three alternate provisions you can use. And if you go beyond that, ask for our help." So what that does is it creates a very collaborative relationship and reduces the degree of tension. It has the added benefit of reducing contracting cycle times by a measurable amount and getting deals done faster. So having that EQ is really important. How do you build a relationship and know what their motivating factors and incentives are, rather than just mine, as the leader of a legal department?

At a number of companies, Sabatino had responsibility for procurement in addition to his role in the legal function. This gave him the ability to problem-solve not just for a single department, but for the business as a whole.

It was great because I could get everyone together and say, "How are we going to make this better? Where are the sticking points? Where are the things that don't work?" It's not just about drafting a contract. It's also understanding the process of how things happen, and then tracking metrics to prove the theory.

While working for Schering-Plough, Sabatino saw that the law department was getting dinged for slowing down the procurement process around contracts, namely IT and computer contracts. "It's always getting stuck in the law department" was sort of the thing he heard.

I discovered that contracts would sit in the law department for two days, sit in the finance department for five, and sit in somebody's IT desk for nine. From there, I started asking questions. Where's the problem here, and what are the systems and processes we need to put in place?

Success and efficiency can be directly attributed to the systems and processes you put in place to make these things run smoothly. More often than not, these tests don't run themselves. People have to run them. Putting in place a set of processes allows the strategic business enabler to conjoin their soft skills with their process-oriented mindset, and produce quantifiable results that show true progress is being made thanks to Legal Operations' intervention.

The Metrics Corporate Tour

Tommie Tavares-Ferreria, a longtime GenO practitioner with countless experience in the industry, believes collecting these data and metrics can take you around the entirety of the company.

As a strategic problem solver, sometimes you find yourself going around the whole business. A lot of time is spent socializing with people, meeting with heads of departments, and people that might be stakeholders. The biggest takeaway is always learning. "What are the pain points? What are you trying to achieve here? How do I get the legal and compliance expertise out of our department and to you best?"

Asking questions is only the first step. From there, implementing a strategy or plan to integrate what you've learned into your practice is crucial for sustaining the knowledge you've acquired in the first place, she says.

After the learning and listening, you take it all back to the lab, structuring it in a way that could be prioritized. Then you say to the GC, "This is what I've heard, this is how I think we approach it. This is the money I think I need. These are the results I think we can achieve. And tell me what you're giving a thumbs-up and a thumbs-down to."

Tavares-Ferreira suggests being diligent and keeping your end goal in mind: optimizing the work day to achieve a further level of efficiency.

> There are a plethora of possibilities. Some of it gives you really great ideas, and some of it makes you want to go rip your own stuff out and get new stuff. But seeing what the marketplace is and staying fresh on it is incredibly important. First, it's just all about building out the foundation, being able to seed data and metrics. Then you ask questions. "How much are we intaking, and what category is it coming in?" Then you utilize that data for resource planning.

Having a data- and metrics-based foundation is a key element of how legal operations as a function is now executed. The GenO professional understands the value of time, especially in contract lifecycle management. Metrics is an evaluation of what is already there, like an analysis of all the current systems and processes in a company. For a business, saving money and time are the biggest indicators of success.

With that being said, sometimes trends, metrics, and measurements are attained in a less traditional, or numerically quantifiable, method. Working experience provides a useful metric in determining what works and what doesn't in a company.

Testing Your Theory in the Workplace

Connie Brenton is Founder and CEO of LegalOps.com. Brenton gained an understanding of how efficiency played a part in her understanding the importance of implementing metrics based on life and work experience. For instance, when corporations started to outsource certain legal tasks to offshore vendors, she was determined to discover just how effective such a tactic would be. She headed to India to do her own evaluations.

Before, nobody felt comfortable moving legal work to anyone other than an attorney. Now you're talking about moving it to an attorney based in India, so prove it to me. The things that the trips to India showed me were the process controls, the security controls, the end-to-end thoughtfulness around creating new technology that they were using there.

Brenton's work in India also helped reveal differences in processes that could be carried over to her organization and its practices back home to improve them.

There was also a time when I was visiting another Indian facility with the owner, and he went to take some documents out with us. They wouldn't let him go, because they had a process. You cannot leave the building with this type of documentation, regardless of who you are. It was really interesting—an aha moment.

Brenton's work brought her back to the United States, where she began to notice the differences in working culture. Her trips to India were a nontraditional way of collecting metrics regarding efficiency and process. Perspective is oftentimes the key to understanding the level of change that needs to be implemented based on the metrics and measurements that you've collected. The challenge with implementing change based on metrics is that means someone's job is going to be redefined significantly, she says.

Legal Ops has a responsibility to help members of the company understand how their jobs will change, and making sure that they understand how that's positive for the enterprise and for them individually is extremely important.

These implementations are not something that can be taken care of and understood with just one conversation. It's something that has to be established through a process of learning and communicating. This includes being in communication with the entire chain of command when implementing a metrics-based change. It is tantamount to include both the individuals that are impacted, as well as their managers and team leaders.

Discussing details, expectations, and the payoff for implementing change will create transparency between departments. This will not only help them understand the big picture and motivation behind any changes, but also how everyone involved in the process will benefit, Brenton says.

> It's not what they're just going to stop doing tomorrow, but it's how they're going to reuse that time to do other things that are more valuable to the enterprise. It's very important to this journey.

Waste Management

A lot of times, data and metric collecting shines light on inefficiencies in the business. Kyle Mcneil, Contracts Lifecycle Management Practice Leader at EY Law, describes the process by which technology moves the spotlight to areas of waste, both in time and money. Waste is not to be confused with the continuous improvement process, which is an incremental fine-tuning of an established and effective process. Waste is literally a poor use of the enterprises time and/or money that needs to be excised, not honed. It may well be an entire process that simply needs to be sunsetted. To Mcneil, creating efficiency in the workflow means eliminating waste wherever possible.

> There's plenty of waste in the contracting process and enterprises. If you can, you should identify it, and put a value to it from a time-and-money perspective. Find errors that are related to noncompliant activities. There's always opportunities to improve, steps to eliminate, or legal content to streamline in order to make processes efficient.

Though each situation is different and must be assessed based on the company, employees, and financial capacity, oftentimes, creating an additional step in the process of your workflow can halt efficiency.

> What is all the activity that happens between the starting point and the ending point? I think of it as waste. I just think of it as pure waste. Waste of your time, waste of the counterparty's time. The earlier you can eliminate a process, the better downstream.

What does this mean to individuals whose work may be changed on a day-to-day basis? Initially, there likely will be pushback. How do you tell someone that a perhaps significant part of what they do each day will no longer be done? Put yourself in the shoes of an in-house lawyer. Your workload is already more than you could possibly get done on a given day. That's the perpetual state of an in-house law department. So you are going to change how they do what they do. You may be adding what appear to be new additional tasks to their plate. But you are eliminating something that you can demonstrate is not contributing as it should to the company's bottom line.

You can produce all the right metrics to justify why something needs to change, but you still need to work with the humans behind the work to help them adapt it to their current working style. They may believe all of the metrics that are presented to them. They may believe executive management when they say this is why it's good for the company. But at the end of the day, they still have to change the way they work, and that takes soft skills and an understanding of their position, goals, and mindset.

Shining a Light on Your Skills

Carrick Craig is Senior Counsel at Miller Canfield. He gives advice on how to avoid certain inefficiencies, and how metrics and data can create opportunities to spot those issues in the first place. Craig describes his experience implementing data and metrics into a useful implementation for his company.

While I was at Western Michigan University, we implemented the contract management system. I was able to give my president a year-end summary of all our data and all our metrics as it related to contracts, who were our most frequent users? What was the dollar value of all the contracts we reviewed? How many, just in terms of raw numbers, did we review? How many man-hours, person-hours, employee-hours would that translate into in the absence of that contract management system?

Now that's using metrics to justify the corporate investment in your Legal Operations department—and laying the groundwork to boost the budget over time! While asking process-related questions may take time initially, this is one of the best methods for understanding the needs of a company, Craig points out.

It gave us a chance to justify our existence. Contract management systems are not inexpensive, they're not a trivial cost. One of the things I wanted to show was they pay for themselves manyfold over in terms of efficiency, the ability to capture all this data, and to really know who's doing what and what the value is to the university.

Data and metrics can be procured in a number of ways. Finding the most efficient methods for collecting this information may create discrepancy or incomplete information. Instead, implement a method that combines your technological capabilities with your end goal, Craig counsels.

If I wanted to find out how many contracts did we review for academic affairs, I would have to send my paralegal—who I'm paying X amount of dollars an hour, ramped up for benefits—to physically go through every file, identify which one is from academic affairs, and try to tally that. That's a labor-intensive process that probably consumes any benefit you would get from it by the work it would take to produce it. Whereas at the end of the first year, I could go to my administrative assistant and say, "Pull up every contract we reviewed in excess of a hundred thousand dollars and let me know how many days it was in the system." Within 45 minutes, I would have a spreadsheet on my desk saying, you reviewed 182 contracts with value more than $100,000. And they spent an average of nine days in the system.

The foundation of your contribution to the big picture is that you are optimizing a business process, and thinking about it and promoting it using metrics, measurements, and management controls. How does one create efficiency? What are your inputs? What are your outputs? What do your stakeholders want? How do you measure value? How do you measure ROI? This is even before you think about automating a process with technology.

'Management Controls'—It's Not What You Think

The phrase "management controls" almost sounds like an oxymoron. It's not about controlling things but it's about putting controls in place in the middle of a process. Let us explain. Let's say that a clause library is being put in place that a business unit can utilize without legal intervention in every negotiation. The clauses in the library can be ranked based on risk to the business. If there's a particular clause that's high risk but used as the first fallback provision 90% of the time, a management control could appear in the form of a report that identifies this usage and allows the legal department to pause the process and ask the business why it defaults to that provision. Do the other two that are lower risk not work or are they trying to accelerate the negotiation by giving up more to the counterparty out of the gate? There's a management control in the process that provides visibility to the legal department without them exercising tight controls over the ability of the business to operate efficiently. Management controls are all about visibility rather than control. They are actually viewed by audit committees as a very sound risk management strategy.[1]

---

1. "Common Risks and Opportunities Audit Committees Should Continue," RSM, June 26, 2023, https://rsmus.com/insights/services/risk-fraud-cybersecurity/common-risks-and-opportunities-audit-committees-should-consider.html.

Understand It to Automate It

Understanding the business process itself allows you to automate any contract management, or any business process for that matter. Understanding the business function is followed by optimizing the business function and deciding the ideal way it should be measured.

In the case of contract management, the best starting point for automating the business process is to create a repository of executed agreements. These should be organized with parent-child relationships, with metadata extracted. This makes it easy to search and retrieve information, but also allows for the extraction of information, helping you to be informed about how to automate the front end of the process.

Having a good understanding of metrics and measurements allows for a cleaner workflow throughout the company. In the world of contract management, time is the most valuable resource. Carrick Craig explains:

> We had a game we used to do called "find the contract, who's got the contract?" Do you have the contract? A single repository was the key. Before that, if I wanted to find all the contracts that related to our health system, our healthcare provider, our onsite clinical facility, I would have to do another physical search and go through. We did have a file system where each contract had a number with it, but it was stored chronologically. If you're spending half your day going through file cabinets, looking for healthcare contracts, you could have written the bill and it wouldn't matter, because you're not going to get to them all, because you're spending all your time on these administrative duties that are just not productive.
>
> The more you can automate that, especially in contract compliance, the better off the institution's going to be. For those that really want to be competitive moving forward, efficiency and making sure you get your return on investment is big. If

I'm going to give you this dollar, tell me what you're going to do with it and tell me why it's a good thing to do. The more metrics, the more control you have over that flow, the better off you are.

You have a better story to tell through data metrics, you're not just hand-waving, you're actually using data and metrics and management controls, and communicating the actual operational impact throughout the company. From there you can begin segmenting work in a strategic way, which not just makes the law department efficient, but enables the General Counsel to say, "Here's how I'm better serving the interests of the organization. I'm consuming the funds that are allocated to the law department in a very strategic way to ensure that the things that are of highest value to the organization are the ones that we're focused on with our in-house people who are actually using their law background to ensure achievement of those objectives in a risk-managed way."

Metrics, measurements, and management controls will make GenO the hero in both the law department and the rest of the enterprise. And that's exactly where you want to be. Mastering the soft skills discussed in the next two chapters will put the finishing touches on all of your hard work.

6

The Power Qualities

Part One—Personal Qualities to Be Mastered

By exercising those soft skills, you're educating yourself, you're making people feel heard, and you're going to learn where the sticking points are, where you can effect change. You're going to connect dots. And at the end of the day, our job is really to make people happy in their jobs, and not frustrated.

STEPH COREY, *CEO and co-founder, UpLevel Ops*

As we have laid out the case for the elevated status of the Legal Operations profession, we have referenced various skills, talents, and qualities required by the role. So far, we have discussed that our GenO hero must be a business-minded process thinker with tech knowledge who understands the legal aspects of the business processes that flow through the enterprise, but also understands the value drivers associated with these processes—risk, cost, revenue, cycle time. One who goes outside the boundaries of the law department to become a strategic business enabler.

Tech-, legal-, financial, and process-minded: Those are the most obvious contributors to the desired DNA. You might call them the hard skills. To complete our profile, we seek an array of qualities and skills that, taken together, create the holistic Legal Ops professional. The implementation of GenO's portfolio across all departments requires more than a knowledge of business documents with legal provisions and their flow through the enterprise.

GenO will be called upon to persuade the people who comprise these departments to work smoothly with them to achieve the desired result. Legal Ops professionals build a network of relationships as well as a workflow and work streams for documents and data. And just as one contract template does not fit all circumstances, they are always ready to read the room as they move forward with an array of skills that take into consideration the complex humanness of those they are asking to work with them.

Just to be clear, these soft skills—which we will refer to as power skills—are every bit as crucial to the GenO persona as are the hard skills. We call them power skills because they have the power to create the relationships GenO will require to truly effect change within the enterprise. They can be learned with practice and finely tuned through experience. We don't believe there are people who are born with soft/power skills and people that simply don't have them. If you don't have the right skill set, it can all be learned.

These skills will be discussed in depth in this and the following chapter.

Reinventing the CLOC Wheel

Our wheel is modeled after the CLOC 12 Core Competencies reference wheel.[1] The Corporate Legal Operations Consortium defines these as follows: "The 12 core competencies represent areas of focus that every legal department must manage to have a disciplined, efficient, and effective legal function. They are also part of a bigger picture: determining legal department maturity. The 12 competencies serve as a benchmark to compare a department's growth to others in the industry."

Many of CLOC's core competencies are management skills, such as financial management, vendor management, knowledge management, and so on. Our 12 Power Skills are more aligned

---

1. Corporate Legal Operations Consortium, "The CLOC 12 Core Competencies Reference Model," https://cloc.org/wp-content/uploads/2018/12/CLOC_CCRM_2018.pdf.

with management of the mind and emotions, as they relate to interpersonal interactions. Our colleagues across departments will be asked to commit time and resources to the project. They will be given to understand that this is a continuous process of improvement, not a one time plug-in never to be revisited. You want them to buy in and become true partners in this initiative. To accomplish that, the soft, or power, skills must be engaged.

We have found that GenO Legal Ops professionals ask themselves: "What do I need to be successful in this interaction? How do I make sure I am putting myself in their shoes?" These types of introspective questions led us to create our Power Skills Wheel for GenO. The wheel serves as a guide or checklist that will ensure we have taken into account the humanness of those we will depend on to help us achieve our goals.

Steph Corey, CEO and co-founder of UpLevel Ops, believes soft skills are a vastly underrated component of great leadership. Soft skills aren't degreed skills, they aren't credentialed skills, or skills that can be demonstrated by metrics. In a way, she says, they are more character traits.

> You can't point to a framed certificate on your office wall and say, "See, I have a degree in kindness." So in terms of leadership skills, we call them soft skills. Some might call it a feminine trait. You just don't hear it discussed a lot in terms of leadership, but that's exactly what leadership is. And it's getting to really understand what's happening with each individual person, what's happening within each function, and then bringing consensus, getting them to a point of consensus so that you can all move forward. I mean, think about what a better place we would all be in if every leader acted that way and we would all be feeling like we're on the same team.
>
> I encourage Legal Ops managers and professionals to really get out there. You're the face of Legal in many ways. You're the one who is interacting across all of the business lines and func-

tions. Just hanging out with people in different departments is a really important function and position for Legal Ops managers to take. And it's also a way to expand your profile and learn about the other functions and how the company works in general. It'll just give you a different view.

So let's dig in. We will take you around the wheel, with input from our panel of experts. We think you'll find that it's not as intimidating an undertaking as it may appear at first glance. You will identify the soft skills you already possess, and will gain insight into mastering those that may seem to be outside your wheelhouse.

The Power Qualities and Skills of GenO Success

Our list is divided into two categories: Qualities and Skills. Qualities are the more emotion-driven elements; Skills are more process-oriented, and more objectively measurable.

Qualities

1. Empathy
2. Patience
3. Kindness
4. Pure intent
5. Morale Maven
6. Adaptability

Skills

7. Explaining in primary colors/large numbers
8. Leading from the back
9. Humble self-promotion
10. Rapid decision-making
11. Consensus mindset
12. Radical transparency

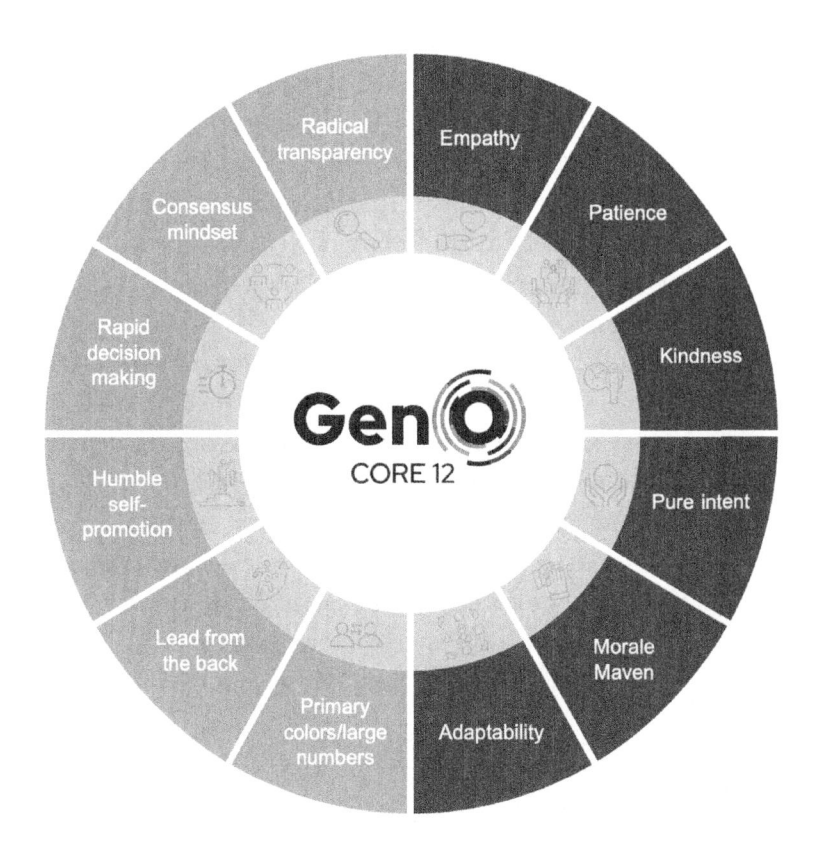

Quality 1: Empathy—the headwaters of power qualities

Don't make assumptions about another person's challenges, limitations, and motivations.

The often-frenetic pace of work experienced by GenO professionals causes some to view their business objectives as paramount, assuming they will automatically receive support from their colleagues for their initiatives. That assumption, by itself, will often prove to be false. Empathy is a good starting point to achieve the desired support.

Empathy is one of the most powerful traits of a successful changemaker. Often confused with sympathy, empathy goes deeper. It implies the sharing of a basic, common experience: an illness, job loss, divorce, death of a family member. On the job, you can sympathize with a coworker who is having a hard time with their boss. But empathy arises from a much closer shared experience: Do you keep running up against a brick wall every time you attempt to streamline document flow? No one is listening? Yes, I have been there and I know your pain. Together we can solve this.

To cultivate the empathy needed to do your job in Legal Ops, you have to get inside the skins (and hearts) of those in the departments with whom you will be working. You must bring multiple power skills into play: listening, patience, direct communication, kindness. You can sympathize with someone else almost immediately. Developing empathy for someone else happens only over time and with an intention of getting inside their hearts. Only then can you identify the right path to consensus building and acceptance.

If you have true empathy for your internal clients, they will experience it and will reward you with acceptance and cooperation.

Bob Mignanelli, VP of Legal Strategy/Operations, Digital & Technology, & Procurement for Haleon (formerly GSK Consumer Health, maker of brands such as Theraflu, Advil, Emergen-C, Tums, and ChapStick), offers an overview of the value—the critical importance—of having empathy when seeking to collaborate with people across the enterprise.

> Empathy, to me, is the ability to look at a situation or an objective from your business colleagues' perspective. It is incredibly important. Because if you don't do that, you won't truly understand what they're trying to achieve and why they're trying to do it. But also, if you do that, it may change your view on certain things too. It may change your view on how you approach them. It is so critically important because when you can do

that, when you can have empathy, when you can collaborate, when you've honed those interpersonal skills, then you're able to work as a team a lot better.

For our Legal Operations colleagues, establishing that empathy will allow you to drive initiatives where you'll get into situations where the overall goal may be the same, but the drivers and the individual stakeholder objectives may be slightly different and sometimes at odds. And it's hard. It's the hardest part of the job. It really is.

Mike Haven, Head of Global Legal Operations for Intel Corporation, discourses on the "empathy quotient" that he says is essential for Legal Ops to carry out its role as efficiency expert across all departments.

EQ, the empathy quotient, is a really important soft skill to have in this role. Because you have to really sort of feel the pain of the parts of the department and understand, from their point of view, why this problem needs to be solved and should be a priority. And so, having empathy, and listening and understanding and developing empathy, and then maybe even having compassion in some cases, has to happen.

Donovan Bell, Director of Information and Contract Experience (Global Legal Operations) for Intel, reflects back on the elementary school playground dynamic to explain how one develops empathy for groups. In this case he substitutes emotional intelligence for EQ, but it's the same concept.

Emotional intelligence is that ability to recognize and understand the emotions in yourself and others, and the ability to use this awareness to manage your behavior and your relationships. I'm going to take us back to elementary school. It's recess, right? You're running and playing, you're having to deal with a lot of different personalities, a lot of different experiences and a lot of different emotions. So many different dynamics. Am I going to be the last kid picked on the kickball team?

The exhilaration of the monkey bars and going through those aspects and those types of things. You are constantly gauging, "How are my emotions handling things? And how am I keeping that in check?" So likewise, when you think of those dynamics of self-awareness, self-management, your social awareness, and your relationship management, that comes into play when any economic or situational conditions come to fruition within your company that impact many people.

And so you're constantly checking yourself, but also taking stock and inventory of how everyone else is feeling. I think that's at the core of it: understanding how people are feeling, and understanding how you're feeling, and being able to make those adjustments accordingly.

Empathy: When you are able to be truly empathetic, a connection will be established that will serve you well as you embed yourself in the organization.

Quality 2: Patience—tough to practice, worth the effort

Learn your organizational speed limit and how it varies from one department to another. Be patient as you understand these variations.

Patience, like empathy, cannot be strictly defined. How much is enough? How much is too little or too much? Savants will say one can never be sufficiently patient. But in the business world, we have our limits with patience. The drumbeat of deadlines and the need to realize revenue can cultivate a culture of impatience.

The GenO practitioner needs to cultivate their own culture of patience. Your instinct is to thrust your perfect solution to a document traffic jam on the parties involved. You have vetted it, you know it will work. What's the holdup? But if we are unwilling, or unable, to wait for the timing of an event to be right, we risk losing any advantage that might be gained by rushing ahead. Caution: We are not advocating for passivity; patience can be invoked while still charging ahead deliberately with initiatives.

Remember, you represent change, and change can be threatening on many levels. You are seeking consensus, not forced acquiescence. Patience requires you to proceed in measured steps: Get to know the parties and their pain points. Gauge their tolerance for change. Find out who the true deciders are, and make sure you have convinced them of the efficacy of the solution. Understand that despite the apparent logic of a decision there may also be political (or budgetary) factors that need to be incorporated. For those who tend to be strangers to patience, the investment in time can be initially excruciating. Once you have been through the process a few times, you begin to get a handle on how much patience will be required to achieve the desired outcome. Patience also gives clarity of thought. How many times have we heard the phrase, "time can provide perspective, and reflection can bring clarity."

Tommie Tavares-Ferreira discusses the importance of taking your time to learn about a company's culture, its traditions, its pain points, by embarking on an intentional learning tour. This she undertook when she started her job as Senior Corporate and Commercial Counsel at healthcare payment platform provider Cedar Cares, Inc. She spent four months on her "learning and listening tour."

> It was going around the whole business. It was socializing with people, meeting with heads of departments, and deputies, and people that might be my biggest stakeholders and learning, "What are the pain points? What are you trying to achieve here? How do I get the legal and compliance expertise out of our department and to you in the best way?" Then taking all that back to the lab, sort of structuring it in a way that could be prioritized, saying to the GC, "This is what I've heard, this is how I think we approach it. This is the money I think I need. And tell me what you're giving a thumbs-up and a thumbs-down to. Do we have alignment? OK, great."

So I want to see what's out there. And some of it gives you really great ideas, and some of it makes you want to go rip your own stuff out and get new stuff. But it's about wanting to just see what the marketplace is and staying fresh on it. That takes time and patience. You have to set aside time for that.

Kyle Mcneil, Contracts Lifecycle Management Practice Leader at EY Law, begins the consensus-building process by creating a value statement that will be presented to the stakeholders. The barriers and lost opportunities may be obvious to the Legal Ops veteran. But for those in the law department and the other impacted departments, the logjams may be hidden behind a wall of accepted process.

There's plenty of waste in the contracting process and enterprises. But you should identify that waste, you should put a value to it from a time, from a money perspective. You should also identify errors that are related to noncompliant activities that may be occurring, the identifiers of waste. You can really clearly point out that there's opportunities to improve, eliminate steps, streamline things, streamline legal content in order to streamline processes, things like that. But you have to take the time to create your case.

Remember, the challenge is that someone's job is going to change significantly and a lot of times it's the in-house lawyer's job that's going to change significantly. So helping our clients understand how their jobs will change, and making sure that they understand how that's positive for the enterprise and for them individually, is extremely important. This is change management at its very basic, and it's not something you can do in one conversation. It's something that has to happen through a process of learning and tailoring messages and communicating that down to the individuals that are impacted and involving their leaders in those communications. It's not what they're just going to stop doing tomorrow, but it's how they're going to reuse that time to do other things that are more valuable to the enterprise. Patience is very important to this journey.

GenO Legal Ops professionals should consider the multi-disciplinary nature of contract management and other enterprise initiatives often driven by legal, taking care to understand and appreciate the different organizational speed limits in each department when driving timelines and deliverables. Identify their priorities and build these into your project timelines.

Patience: The habit of knowing when the moment for acceptance of change has arrived.

Quality 3: Kindness—being gentle with the truth

To 'be kind' has become somewhat of a cliché phrase. As GenO leaders transition to become strategic business enablers, it is critical that they are kind.

"Kindness" ranks among the English language's most abused and misunderstood terms. Of late, kindness as a concept has sometimes been weaponized. If someone is referred to as unkind, they are instantly assumed to be behaving undesirably. As such, it is critical to understand what kindness is and invoke it in one's own behavior rather than use it to judge others.

Kindness is not compassion—but it should be offered with compassion. Nor should kindness be confused with empathy—one can be kind without truly sharing or understanding another's experience. Again, kindness flows more easily from an empathetic mindset. Kindness invokes a way of doing—with sensitivity to the needs of others who may be unprepared to follow your lead.

The notorious gangster Al Capone reportedly said, "Don't mistake my kindness for weakness. I am kind to everyone, but when someone is unkind to me, weakness is not what you are going to remember about me." While instances of true kindness on Capone's part do not fill volumes, his differentiation of "kind" and "weak" rings true.

How do we define "kind" in the context of our GenO Legal Ops professionals? It is the ability to interact with an internal client—or even a law department team member—in such a way that difficult information is shared honestly but with compassion. The Legal Ops professional's job is that of changemaker, for the good of the enterprise. This more often than not involves changes in a process or role that others may be reluctant to accept. You have done your research and concluded that the changes must be made. Delivering the news with kindness will increase the likelihood of a positive response. It requires one to be thoughtful, considerate of others, aware of how one's actions and words may land on the other.

This does not imply you are sugarcoating the news. As Capone noted, kindness does not come from a place of weakness. Just because you act in a kindly fashion does not mean you will back down from your decision. "Firm but fair" might well describe your attitude. So often in corporate life, people remember how decisions were handed down to them. Be kind, and you will be remembered, if not fondly, at least not as insensitive. As a reminder, your goal is ultimately to be your true self and express kindness, because it is how you would like to be treated. It is not being suggested simply as a way to "choreograph" your behavior to accomplish an objective. Kindness is not a means to an end. It is an end in itself. This is an important distinction. Being kind while also genuine is critical.

UpLevel Ops' Steph Corey had previously joined Hewlett-Packard's legal team during a time of growth by acquisition. The acquired firms had, among other assets, their own legal departments. Emotions ran high as consolidation occurred among the many entities. Corey, as a newbie with less experience than many on her team, could have been traumatized by the experience. But her HP colleagues treated her with excessive kindness, guiding her through the chaotic period with consideration.

I go back to my days at HP where I felt so overwhelmed. This very young person joining this very seasoned team of lawyers—I had no idea what their day-to-day was like, and so how do I support them? And it's scary and overwhelming; I think I was very lucky to be in a place where I could watch all of this in an environment that was very supportive, and the attorneys all took time to train me. I sat with every deputy general counsel there, and they taught me about their organization, IP and litigation and commercial and all of that. So I was really fortunate to not be thrown to the wolves. There was a structure there, and so I was able to learn.

I'm sure a lot of new Legal Ops managers feel the same way when they enter their roles. But you're not doing this in a vacuum, and you certainly shouldn't be doing this in a vacuum. So the good news is, if you take a few minutes to talk to the lawyers, they'll help you. I think we've lost a lot of that in corporate America today. You join a role, everybody's just working their tails off. They're so crazy, and you're drinking from a fire hose from Day One. And it wasn't like that at HP. HP really took its time to train its employees, and people took time to mentor.

Corey took that lesson to heart. Today, as a consultant, when her team is called upon to facilitate a potentially difficult transition, she reminds her colleagues to be patient and kind as the process moves forward.

Kindness: The ability to be thoughtful, considerate, and compassionate during difficult circumstances.

Quality 4: Pure intent—a communications foundation

When interacting with others, assume pure intent on their part and assume they feel the same about you.

Honing one's craft in a law department is a great foundation for Legal Ops to build functional/technical skills. However, there is a tendency to "question everything," and trust when there is evidence that something/someone can be trusted. Legal training is based on risk avoidance, so this is natural.

When leading enterprise initiatives such as contract management, it is critical that GenO professionals approach interactions with colleagues with a trust model based on pure intent. This is not only a "positive mindset" but is also expedient. It enables GenO to fully immerse themselves into listening and learning, rather than questioning. A pure-intent mindset will also create a positive perception of the legal department—a group that has a history of being (mis)perceived as the "department of no."

As you establish a reputation throughout the enterprise of assuming pure intent on the part of others, your internal clients will respond in a like manner. The relationship then begins with trust, rather than waiting for it to be proven. Instead, your interactions will be based on "I trust you until you show me that I should not." That is where you want to be operationally. To do this, you may need to consciously shake off the old legal habit of self-preservation and protection. Let go of suspicion. Instead, assume you can safely do the work that needs to be done.

Gerald Wright, former leader of the Global Contract Solutions Group at Intel and now retired, found early on in his Legal Ops incubation that nondisclosure agreements were stacking up in Legal. He directly addressed the issue, and took responsibility for fixing it.

> With my experience in doing all of that, I said, "Well, where are the deficiencies? Where does the department and where do the business—where can they use the most help?" And I went to our leadership and I said, "We're way behind in NDAs. … We do a lot of NDAs in this company. We can be more efficient at doing [them]." And nobody owned it. And so I said, "I'm going to own it." And so I took over NDAs. Initially … the law department didn't see a need, but … I just did it anyway. I saw

the need. And one of the things at Intel, and I'm sure with lots of large organizations, is [that] we have this saying, "You own your own employment."

And so I took that to heart and I said, "OK. Leadership says maybe [it doesn't] see the need for that." ... At their level, that was their thought. But at my level, what I've been doing in my career at the company, I've seen the inefficiencies. And I said, "Well, I think we do need it." And I just pushed on, and it's an amazing program today. ... We've driven so much efficiency [that] it takes probably five to ten minutes to get an NDA signed now. When I started, it was ten to fifteen days.

If you lead with pure intent, you will be repaid with pure intent.

Quality 5: Morale Maven—pumping up the players

Legal Operations professionals need to focus on maintaining team morale in the face of adversity.

Initiatives are often delayed and may face budget cuts. Further, enterprise initiatives championed by Legal Ops are still in their infancy and may be met with natural skepticism. This could result in team attrition/reorganization or changes in the approach or scope.

The Morale Maven responds by leveraging the principles of candor and radical transparency. GenO professionals should proactively outline the realities of the "shifting sands" to their teams. They should create an environment where every team member can quickly pivot and adapt if necessary. Connect with team members (within Legal Ops as well as other groups) individually and see how they're feeling. A high degree of empathy is necessary for this.

It is imperative to maintain high morale as Legal Ops works its magic throughout the enterprise. This applies not only to the initial implementation of the practices and processes that will ensure your team's success as business enablers. For the work is ongoing, a matter of continuous improvement as outlined many decades ago by W. Edwards Deming, prophet of quality improvement in modern industry.[2]

The motivational role of the GenO leader applies to the Legal Ops team as well as its internal clients. As our interviewees have indicated, the work can be difficult. The team frequently encounters pushback from those expected to adapt to a new system. Too, the systems do not always perform as advertised out of the gate. This creates another layer of frustration.

The Morale Maven must keep eyes on the prize at all times. This calls for a deep and true well of enthusiasm for reaching the goal, and it must be effectively imparted or you'll find yourself far out in front of the dispirited troops.

Intel's Donovan Bell discusses the fine art of ongoing motivation of the Legal Ops team. We asked him: How do you keep people energized? How do you make sure they're not demoralized? What happens when times get tough and the pressure increases?

> A safe, skilled, agile framework principle is unlocking the intrinsic motivation of your knowledge workers, right? So identify those areas where you're able to find those motivators. Is it recognition? Is it affirmation? Is it acknowledging wins? Is it condensing the work that you're doing and finding small wins so that you can create continual successes?
>
> It is a matter of having a mantra of relentless improvement in everything that you're doing. And you must hold yourself accountable to it. ... The best trait is that authenticity, that being vulnerable ... being open to the reality that these are some tough times, challenging times, but here is our opportunity. And in the context of that opportunity here, here's how we can find quick wins. That is how your team makes the transition from problem solvers to business enablers.

---

2. The W. Edwards Deming Institute, "Viewing the World Through a Different Lens," https://deming.org/learn/about-dr-deming.

Then it becomes a matter of continuing to let your team know: Here's the impact that we're having on the broader vision and the goal, here's how we're enabling business. If you're on the sales side of contracting, if you're able to make that process more efficient, streamlined, then you're able to obtain that revenue even faster. If you're on the buy side and you're able to again streamline that process, shortcut that process, then you're able to achieve that savings or that deal in a shorter time frame, so you're able to really maximize the value of that.

When you find those wins, you highlight that heavily, you celebrate that continually. ... That's a real key to both maximizing the motivation of your team [and] demonstrating the value to your leadership.

You'll go through some challenging times, especially when you're told the budget's cut and now you need to do more, but we're not going to increase your staff. You have to figure out a way to continue to find value. And so you have to learn that yes, that's a tough message, but how do I spin this to ... an opportunity? ... And that opportunity [is] where we shine.

At the same time, how do you motivate senior executives to keep this initiative on their radar, so that they understand the ROI of this, such that it's not something that takes a backseat in tight times? To share your motivation and enthusiasm skills with the executive leadership team, the challenge is a bit more complex, Bell says.

You kind of have to play that three-level chess where you're motivating up: You're communicating up the value; you're helping your leadership look good from that aspect; and then you're finding that fulfillment in these small wins and showing how your team excels from that standpoint.

It actually dovetails with another of our 12 Power Skills: humble self-promotion. You must constantly share your achievements with executive leadership to maintain high morale on their part for your strategies. But share in such a way that they, too, can claim credit for your success. Keep sharing and keep smiling!

The Morale Maven motivates by sharing wins and reiterating your shared long-term objectives.

Quality 6: Adaptability—be responsive to your environment

Just like EQ, or emotional quotient, GenO Legal Operations professionals will be measured on their AQ, or adaptability quotient.

Since Legal Operations is where "GC aspirations are turned into action," GenO professionals will be thrust into new domains that are relatively undefined, and broadly impacted. As such, GenO professionals will need to know how to quickly adapt and pivot, reshuffle priorities as needed, and learn entirely new domains.

GenO Legal Operations will go into a new domain, interact with new groups and constituencies by first understanding before trying to be understood. One must learn the "language" of these new groups as well as the rhythm and cadence of management and communication. Then, utilize this learning to seamlessly transition into and between initiatives that may be "first time" initiatives for the company or for Legal Ops. One note: Be prepared to pivot if initial forays into these initiatives do not bear fruit.

The ideal candidate for a Legal Ops role will be that person who loves to innovate, says co-author Prashant Dubey. They are invigorated by the challenge of finding solutions to complex kinks in the process.

> If you are someone who believes in one-size-fits-all solutions, Legal Ops is not for you. The GenO professional must be a master of adaptability, of open-mindedness, of flexibility. Your solutions and processes may be driven by technology, but their success remains tied to the vagaries of human behavior. An

elixir for cost-savings and streamlining in one department may fall flat in the next. So be prepared for anything.

In addition to the peculiarities of departmental human culture across the enterprise, you will encounter in-built environment challenges. Something as basic as the location of workers in today's hybrid workplace must be considered. Where are the documents being written, reviewed, edited, shared? Are sensitive legal documents being whisked outside the information technology firewall? Then we find that many variations of the internal document management architecture exist from department to department. We hate Google Docs, we love Google Docs, we do everything in Dropbox, spreadsheets rule, or they don't … If you haven't done so yet, sign up now for advanced yoga courses. You'll need them.

Cedar's Tommie Tavares-Ferreira spoke to us about the value—and the risk—of having a playbook to guide one through the Legal Ops process.

> The playbook is this: Don't presume that your playbook is the right fit for where you're stepping into. At least that's been my playbook. My playbook has been, "There's a solution for all of it." And probably, the solution is the same no matter where you are. But you may have to adapt it to a particular situation.
>
> For example, I want to know how much money I spend on outside firms. I'd like to save money with those firms, and how do I go about doing that? The playbook is that you should probably put in an e-billing solution. You should probably put in outside counsel guidelines. When you get big enough, you should probably build out a panel and then have a process for how you select, etc., etc. You should probably figure out what percentage of that you want to be alternative to firms.
>
> And so I think there is a playbook. But inside of that playbook, there's also this "Don't use the playbook until you actually can figure out where you plug-and-play that." Meaning the tooling that you used at the last place may not be a right fit for this.

Tavares-Ferreira does not like to adapt on the fly if it can be avoided. Her practice has been to take a "learning tour" of a new company or client prior to making any recommendations.

> So even though you may believe you have the solution for the problem in hand, I think you still go on that learning tour to see, "What am I dealing with here?" I know that I have to put in, for example, an e-billing solution. But is the one I have in mind, or maybe the one I did last time? Is that the right one for this company? And if not, why?
>
> ... No matter what you do—even if you do have a playbook, elements of it—I think you detract from it, because you do want to approach the company. ... Know the business, know what's happening. You want to approach it from that very business-centric sense of "How am I solving your specific problems?" Not the job I had last time, and the money I had last time, and the tooling I had, but how am I solving your specific problems? So I think that that's right. And it's that soft skill of listening, of hearing what people actually need and what they don't need.

Intel's Mike Haven shared his observations on this critical skill from the GenO's leadership role during an interview. "Be ready to pivot!" sums up his advice.

> We talk about AQ, what I call the adaptability quotient. We have to be flexible. We have to be nimble. We have to be adaptable. At Intel, for example, we use OKRs, or "objectives and key results," for all of our goal-setting. And sometimes, in operations, that can be a challenge. Because if you set some annual OKRs, the chances of those OKRs looking the same at the end of the year are almost none, because priorities change, things change. You may be in flight with something and have to go a different direction.

... We're always ready to pivot if necessary, as we're moving along on our roadmap. But our roadmap and our mission remain constant, as far as the high-level objectives we're trying to achieve in our program. ... We have to remain adaptable to keep that big picture in mind at the same time. One's ability to adapt to changing environments in the Legal Ops role determines, as in nature, the extent to which one will evolve.

Now we have reviewed the half dozen personality traits that contribute to the rise of the successful GenO practitioner: empathy, patience, kindness, pure intent, Morale Maven, and adaptability. Let us move on to the other six—which are, perhaps, more easily acquired but every bit as important.

7

The How-To Power Skills

Part Two—With these skills, you will be able to take action to move your initiative forward

When I went back to business school, I learned that the success of any project or objective in business depends on those soft skills—the ability of everybody inside to collaborate and do that well, and to do it efficiently.

> BOB MIGNANELLI, *VP, Legal Strategy/Operations, Digital & Technology, & Procurement, Haleon*

In the previous chapter, we examined six powerful qualities that can build effective interpersonal relationships between GenO and others throughout the enterprise. Those half-dozen, along with the ones we will discuss in this chapter, are the components of our version of the CLOC 12 Core Competencies reference wheel developed by the Corporate Legal Operations Consortium. Now we will look at a set of skills that are more about doing than being. These skills can be more easily mastered, but their significance is no less than our "being" qualities in terms of outcomes.

Our list is as follows:

Qualities (Chapter 6)

1. Empathy
2. Patience
3. Kindness
4. Pure intent
5. Morale Maven
6. Adaptability

Skills (Chapter 7)

7. Explaining in primary colors/large numbers
8. Leading from the back
9. Humble self-promotion
10. Rapid decision-making
11. Consensus mindset
12. Radical transparency

In this chapter, the focus is on 7 through 12, the skills that are focused on shaping group dynamics as well as creating a persona for the Legal Ops team. Because Legal Ops intersects with so many other departments internally and, in addition, with external stakeholders, we want to ensure that its interstitial process does not get lost in the shuffle. The task is to create a face of Legal Ops—to elevate Legal Ops to a GenO, strategic business enabler status within the enterprise.

How is this done? By demonstrating what the GenO team can do on a consistent basis due to the nature of its work ethic, standards, and commitment to business outcomes. Mastering the skills in this chapter will elevate the team's reputation for contributing to the bottom line, while freeing GenO's clients from rote tasks to take on more significant challenges. Thus, GenO gains a reputation for strategic thinking, consensus-building, clear communications, and transparency that guarantees the team will have the attention of corporate leadership. Legal Ops will be proactive about reporting its results back to the top echelon, as well as humbly soliciting testimonials from satisfied clients. That feedback loop comes in handy when it is time to set the budget for the department.

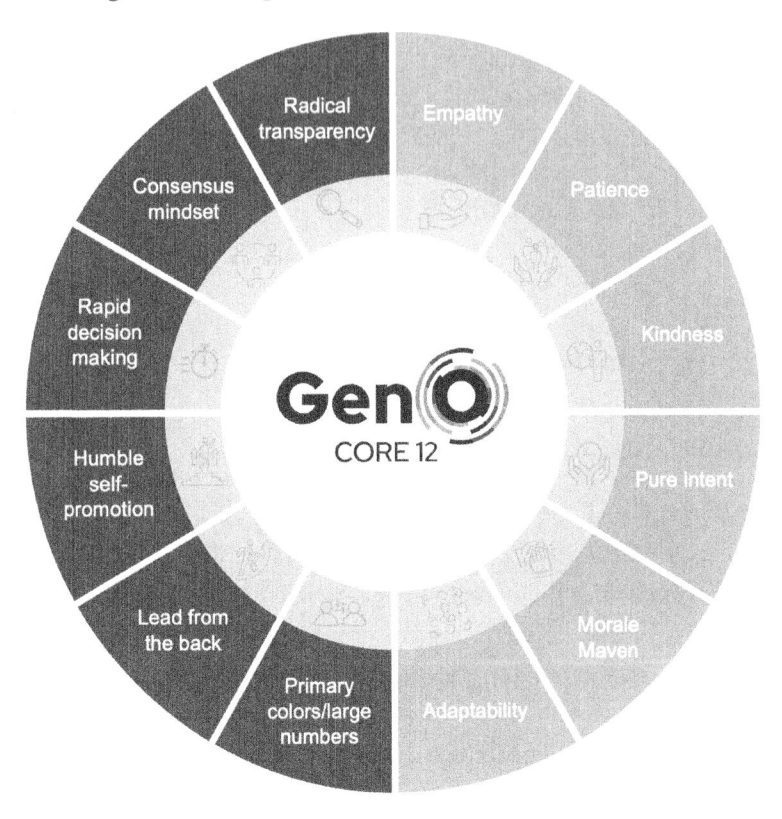

Skill 7: Primary colors/large numbers—keep it simple

As with any domain-specific language, Legal Operations parlance can be hard to decipher for nonlegal colleagues. Communication should be focused on the "least common denominator" and be as understandable as 'primary colors and large numbers.'

When speaking in primary colors and large numbers, in essence the question "What's in it for the client?" is being asked. Part of that includes explaining to the client, "Let me tell you what's in it for you, but let me also walk you through how we're going to do this in an absorbable way so it doesn't overwhelm you." To do this, GenO professionals should default to standard business communication language that is department- or group-agnostic. As strategic business enablers, GenO leaders need to simplify interdepartmental communication so that the legal department is more "accessible" and broadly understood.

One way to test for this is to hold multidisciplinary team meetings and use materials that can be understood by attendees and others even without narrative explanation. Leverage the company's marketing communication resources in advance to ensure that inclusive language is being used.

Gerald Wright, who formerly led the Global Contract Solutions Group at Intel Corporation and is now retired, created a training program to help business departments better understand how to work more efficiently with legal. Much of it involved simple changes business could make in documents and training materials before they went to Legal Ops for review. When the information was delivered in a language/idiomatic-neutral manner, free of the usual legal jargon, Wright received enthusiastic reviews from attendees.

> The business executives, the engineers, the marketing professionals that joined the classes—they wanted to move fast. But they weren't sure how to do it. Part of it was communications-based. We emphasized the benefits to them from the beginning. I said, "What's in it for you?" That matters so much for our user adoption of our CLM [contract lifecycle management] solution. What is in it for the people that are actually going to be utilizing the solution?

Wright's internal classrooms brought Legal Ops together with the rest of the corporation to discuss in straightforward terms the pain points, the bottlenecks, the array of solutions, and the requirements for improving the flow of legal documents. Department personnel would ask, "Why does it take so long for Legal to review a contract?" Legal Ops could respond, "Because the way your team creates the document causes unnecessary language to be included that forces a longer review process." Then the parties could discuss specific ways to streamline their interactions, in language both parties understand.

The same communications theory can be applied to other areas: the budget (Here's how much we need to do this); projections (We can reduce turnaround time or cost/contract by this much); staff requirements (We can accomplish this much faster with this number and type of new hires); and timelines (It will take this many days/weeks to implement this process). By keeping things simple, clear, and easily understood by all parties, GenO facilitates the process of demystifying what it does that contributes to the smooth flow of information, data and documents across the enterprise.

Primary colors and large numbers represent a universal and absorbable language throughout the enterprise. Ferret out all legal jargon and terms of art—in fact, start with a jargon-free team so you become the GenO plain speakers of the business.

Skill 8: Lead from the back—letting the client take charge

When leading initiatives, GenO should identify champions outside Legal Ops early, and include them in leadership roles.

As Generation Operations goes past the boundaries of the legal department and leads enterprise initiatives as a strategic business enabler, there is a temptation to put oneself forward as the leader. This inadvertently causes Legal Ops to be unduly self-focused, sometimes to the detriment of giving other matrix team members visibility. This is learned behavior from years of fighting for recognition amid a department where the hierarchy may be established based on lawyerly seniority. A GenO professional needs to shed this learned behavior and let others "lead" so they can actually get things done by allowing others to also feel a sense of ownership in GenO initiatives that go outside the bounds of the legal department.

GenO professionals should look for opportunities to mentor individuals outside of the legal department. This will enable them to be viewed as "servant leaders"—a term coined by business philosopher Robert K. Greenleaf in his 1970 essay "The Servant as Leader"—which is the mark of a true strategic business enabler.[1]

This can be accomplished through the creation of multidisciplinary teams leveraging talent from departments and groups across the company. As these teams become engaged, you will be able to identify individuals who have shown an interest in the initiatives you are championing. Now, look for opportunities to highlight them to leadership. By recognizing their leadership skills (perhaps you have even discovered them), and appealing to and supporting their desire for advancement, you become the "leader from the back."

In 2011, Lizzie Shilliam, who presently heads Vanderbilt University's legal department but was with Nike at the time, executed this principle by using a book called *Empowered*, written by Josh Bernoff and Ted Schadler (Harvard Business Review, 2010). The book refers to Highly Empowered and Resourceful Operatives (HEROs). Shilliam used it to galvanize an entire army of Nike colleagues to support her mission. She made it *their* mission and gave them ownership—a brilliant strategy that evoked collaboration and raised Legal Ops' profile.

---

1. Robert K. Greenleaf, "The Servant as Leader" (1973 revised edition), https://archive.org/details/20200601-the-servant-as-leader/mode/2up.

Lucy Bassli, founder and principal of InnoLaw Group, PLLC, seeks out these co-leaders and makes sure they get credit when the initiative bears fruit. She avoids branding them as clients of the legal department, which implies an inferior position. She refers to them in terms that reflect a peer-to-peer relationship.

> Say you're working with procurement on a project. Lawyer speak would call them procurement clients. To me, they're my business colleagues, my business counterparts. And they are delighted to be in a leadership role in this journey. I always found they were delighted to provide me with resources, and work with me on this together, as peers, because that's the win-win.

Prashant Dubey, this book's co-author, strongly advises that Legal Ops invests the time to identify and nurture a member of the client team who can co-lead implementation.

> In contract management initiatives, when GenO is attempting to standardize contracting processes to the greatest extent possible, I have found that enabling managers in the business units to take ownership of the standardization is the only way to move the needle without a lot of tumult. In other words, each business unit has a unique contract template or a bespoke contracting process that they can rationalize. Forcing a change (perhaps via leadership edict) to their process (which presumably has worked, albeit inefficiently), can cause consternation. Instead, having an influential representative from the business unit be an active part of the overall implementation team, present their ideas and feel ownership in the overall company's processes usually produces better results. It likely takes a little longer, but will ultimately be more enduring.

Leading from the back does not mean relinquishing your leadership responsibility. Rather, you share the vision with the client/leader, achieve buy-in, and ensure that your client/leader is empowered and rewarded by your shared success.

Skill 9: Humble self-promotion—make sure your work is seen

In balance with "leading from the back," GenO should also ensure that they are promoting progress of their initiatives.

Legal Ops professionals are operationally excellent by training and experience. However, this may result in a "heads down" focus on the project without an accompanying focus on promoting and celebrating project progress and the individuals involved. Because GenO's work spans most of the company's departments and many of its external clients, its process and results can be minimized if it fails to create a persona recognized by the leadership.

GenO professionals should focus on promoting the project and program management components of initiatives they are leading. This can be accomplished by identifying key executive stakeholders whose support needs to be cultivated; by focusing on the "meritocracy" and trusting that program success will be rewarded, while also remembering to highlight your leadership of the program; and by leveraging marketing communications/corporate marketing as appropriate, which can help brand a program that will capture the attention of leaders.

Bob Mignanelli, VP of Legal Strategy/Operations, Digital & Technology, & Procurement at Haleon, advocates blowing one's own horn judiciously, but consistently, so that the department has the attention of the upper echelon.

> Sometimes I think Legal Operations gets put in a corner or maybe viewed as an administrative function. That's not what we want. We want to become a practice area. We want to become a strategic practice area for the department that drives results, and those results are then viewed by the business as, "Hey, look what's going on over there in Legal. Wow! They put in a Legal front door. Look how they're doing intake. Look how they're doing contracts. Look how they've done process refine-

ment and efficiencies. Look at the tech they have. Wow. Look at the reporting and the data."

And that's another really key piece, is that when we get to a point where we're running along and we're yielding data and insights from the operational initiatives that we drive, and we're providing those to our general counsel, then she is able to speak, or [in] my case, he is able to speak to the executive teams in the language of business. So it was no longer, "Oh, Legal's tucked over there" and show what's behind the curtain over there. They're another part of the business and they speak our language and they understand what we're driving. And as operations professionals, we're the engine inside of legal that drives all of that.

Never forget that leadership loves metrics. It's imperative to extract metrics from your work that prove your value—and then share that information on a regular basis with leadership, and with your own team. Carrick Craig, Senior Counsel at Miller Canfield, made it a practice to share key data with his bosses in order to build his team's reputation within the corporation. *(Note: Craig was General Counsel at Western Michigan University but still took core business and GenO principles to cultivate productive relationships with his executive colleagues. Legal Ops is not just for Legal Ops!)*

While I was at Western Michigan University and we implemented our contract management system, I was able to give my president a year-end summary of all our data and all our metrics as it related to contracts: Who were our most frequent users? What was the dollar value of all the contracts we reviewed? How many, just in terms of raw numbers, did we review? How many man-hours, person-hours, employee-hours would that translate into in the absence of that contract management system? It gave us a chance to—and maybe "to justify our existence" is a little bit too dramatic a phrase, but contract management systems are not inexpensive, so they would want to know how it was going. One of the things I wanted to show was they pay for themselves manyfold over in terms of efficiency. So the ability to capture all this data and to really know who's doing what and what the value is to the university was critical to our success.

Tommie Tavares-Ferreira, who runs Legal Ops at Cedar Cares, Inc., believes humble self-promotion is critical for career advancement as well as departmental status. When an internal client sings your praises to the top floor, leadership is going to listen.

Legal Ops is one of these unique and wonderful opportunities where you can really build your career, and build relationships around the entire organization, because we are all about what's in it for them. One of the biggest selling points is saying, for instance, to a salesperson, "I'm going to make this easier, better, faster for you to close deals." I've never heard a salesperson go, "No, I don't think that's a good idea." I mean, that's the endgame. You do that and they'll prop you up on a chair and parade you through the office. So it's a wonderful place to be for visibility, and I think that that's why it's probably one of the reasons why we have seen such an acceleration of folks' careers in this profession, is because of how wide-scale the role is, and the visibility you can get around an entire business from this value prop right here.

Why do we call this humble self-promotion? Because it's not about promoting the individual, but promoting the initiative. If a GenO Legal Ops professional is driving an initiative, it will be recognized by leadership—especially if it is delivering results. Further, as tactical as it may sound, inclusive language such as "We are hoping for the following outcomes and are, in collaboration with our colleagues from sales, procurement, IT, finance, and legal, managing to these outcomes over the next 90 days" is so much more powerful than "This is what I hope to achieve ... ." Yes, yes, there is no "I" in TEAM.

Lawyers and Legal Ops are habituated to avoid self-promotion. Results, they are taught, should speak for themselves. But to humbly and judiciously share the outcomes of Legal Ops initiatives is critical for the department's sustainability, and for its practitioners' career opportunities.

Skill 10: Rapid decision-making—from speed bump to process accelerator

A mark of a successful strategic business enabler is combining data with managerial gut feel to come to quick decisions when at a crossroads.

Many Legal Ops leaders have been trained to defend their decisions with mountains of data. This is particularly true of those with a traditional law school degree. In law school, you are taught to "question everything" and "focus on the facts." When transitioning into a role as a strategic business enabler, the focus needs to be on adding business value, revenue generation, and process efficiency. This requires quick decisions that combine data but also gut instinct.

GenO leaders will become experts in "making decisions with confidence" by observing their environment and knowing what level of data is necessary to rationalize a decision. Some of this will come with experience. It will be useful to create a data framework for decision-making that does not require a tremendous amount of analysis and data gathering to get to a conclusion. Over time, the data sets will shrink as you learn to read the decision-making tea leaves.

Don't be afraid to make mistakes. As a strategic business enabler, it is often better to make a quick decision and have a pathway for rapid remediation if the decision turns out to be the wrong one. As the "leader from the back," GenO can take cues from those clients/leaders who are used to quick decision-making—another good reason to seek out and empower these business partners. You will also find that the outcome-driven business leader accepts that mistakes will be made in the service of moving forward rapidly.

Co-author Prashant Dubey discussed the value of decisiveness on the part of the legal department with Gerald Wright, who at the time was leader of the Global Contract Solutions Group at Intel Corporation but now is retired, during a podcast in 2023. The two agreed that, while lawyers often view rapid decision-making as risky, it is sure to catch the attention of the corner office. At Intel, Wright said, department leaders were expected to "own our own employment." Given that environment, he decided early on that his Legal Ops team would become known for quickly calling the shots.

Wright: *I went to our leadership and I said, "We're way behind in NDAs. We can do NDAs better. We can be more efficient at doing NDAs." And nobody owned it. So I said, "I'm going to own it." And so I took over NDAs. And it's not that there weren't people overseeing NDAs, but it wasn't really a centralized process where there was any kind of automation. We took that on and we automated it. That was my first real entrance into operations where I was supporting clients and their needs, answering questions. I was not involved directly with the business until that point. And frankly, I loved it. It was like now we're solving problems for repeat issues. We're dealing with it at this level vs. we're just answering a question over and over again. We're providing automation that solves problems for all the business units. So I was hooked when I got into that.*

Dubey: *First of all, you have to have a supportive culture that would give you the freedom to raise your hand and say, "I see a business challenge, and I want to own the solution to this." And you got that endorsement. So I would hope that a lot of organizations these days have that kind of culture to empower people that say, "I want* *to solve a business problem." But my guess is, based on how you're articulating it, that function was not even called Legal Operations back in the day, or it wasn't even a function. It was you saying, "I want to solve this problem." So from the start you approached it with an outcomes mindset that calls for making a decision and moving forward.*

Wright: *The leadership didn't see the need that I saw, but I just did it anyway. I saw the need. One reason I felt confident about doing it was that at Intel, and I'm sure with lots of large organizations, "own your own employment" means "if you don't do it, it may never get done." I took that to heart. Leadership maybe doesn't see the need for that. But at my level, I'd seen the inefficiencies. And I said, well, I think we do need it. And I just pushed on, and it's an amazing program today.*

Another part of the decision-making equation is receiving rapid approval for a plan from on high. Tom Sabatino, Executive Vice President and Chief Legal Officer at Rite Aid, advises GenO to have your case completely buttoned up and poised for approval before seeking sanctioning from the bosses.

> What I have found is when you actually can go to a CFO and say to him or her, "Hey, look. We've got a system we want to put in place here that's going to expedite contracts," for example. "We're going to be able to get these contracts faster, we're going to be able to recognize revenue more quickly, we're going to take stuff out of the system that sort of gunks up the works"—they'll say, "OK, where do I write the check?" Which is a great thing to have your CFO tell you. So when you present your case to him or her in an effective way, actually what happens is, the CFO's happy, the lawyers are happy, the businesses are seeing the process expedited so the units are happy. That creates a virtuous cycle for the organization. And then you are able to continue to lift your game for everybody involved. And so I think it's a critical component of what we do.

Rapid decision-making is achieved in part by training the business units to send over requests for approval to the legal department that have already marked most of the appropriate boxes. Dubey says that Legal Ops must take the lead on this setting of expectations by emphasizing the reduction in turnaround time that can be gained when both departments are involved in this streamlining process. Even facilitation of rapid decision-making by others should be internalized by GenO as part of their remit.

> When a business unit sends a contract over for legal review, all of a sudden you're talking about data protection provisions, PII, what are the insurance levels that are needed, and so on—all questions that could be answered ahead of time. We're adding all this time to it, and all of a sudden the business requester of a contract from procurement is saying, "Why is it taking so long?" And we've found that the general counsel and their organization can actually codify some of their legal desires within things like contract templates. They can say, "Let me actually bless a contract template that contains language that I'm comfortable with and empower you, procurement organization, to use fallback provisions and negotiate this on your own. And we'll give you three fallback provisions, in ascending order of risk, that you can use, without legal intervention. And if you go beyond that, ask for our help." So what that does is it creates a very collaborative relationship, reduces the degree of tension, and gets you more quickly to a decision. It has the added benefit of accelerating contracting cycle times and getting deals done faster.

By focusing on the elements that accelerate decision-making, GenO demonstrates that legal can move at the same speed as other business units. This shifts the perception of Legal Operations throughout the enterprise from speed bump to full partner in achieving business outcomes.

Skill 11: Consensus mindset—how to get there

Balancing rapid decision-making with a consensus mindset is critical for a GenO Legal Ops professional.

As GenO transitions into a strategic business enablement mindset, as exemplified above, they need to invoke the Pareto principle (also known as the 80/20 rule and named after Italian sociologist and economist Vilfredo Pareto) to make rapid decisions while still ensuring consensus. From a Legal Operations perspective, the most significant problem to be solved to improve workflow will be obvious. But those in the affected business unit may not have the stomach for it at the outset of the engagement, and so may resist. This is where the GenO leader identifies problems of lower priority in order to begin to build a partnership that will eventually be able to agree to address the key matter.

GenO should identify key supporters/stakeholders in each department, identify their pain points as well as decision criteria, and identify who in the groups have decision rights. This calls upon GenO to be a keen observer in meetings to identify who tends to drive processes and who makes decisions. Next, confirm your understanding with department supporters/stakeholders. Don't be afraid to ask direct questions to identify the decision dynamics and who has decision rights. As described above, Vanderbilt University's Lizzie Shilliam has often invoked the concept of HERO (highly empowered and resourceful operatives) to describe the concept of finding these "ambassadors" in different departments and cultivating them.

> You can't do it all yourself. You need ground troops. You need to cultivate them across the company, and use them to fly your flag and promote your agenda as champions. Let them make decisions even if it's not exactly the decision you would make. Allow them to feel ownership of the process. Build consensus through bringing people along and empowering them, rather than trying to push a program through fiat.

The end result will be that the leaders will make quick decisions but ensure that key stakeholders are "brought along." This is critical as Legal Ops builds credibility within the enterprise for streamlining and enabling business, rather than delaying outcomes.

To be successful in this endeavor, one must master relationship building with one's clients. Sally Guyer, Global Chief Executive Officer at World Commerce & Contracting, has learned that organizations need to start their process by identifying a list of teams, of departments, and of business units that are involved in the process.

> Then you need to start developing the relationship. You need to start listening to them, start understanding what are the pain points, what works well, what doesn't work well. And then I've seen organizations build committees and take that sort of research-based approach internally within their organization to look at opportunities for improvement, all of which goes to the bottom line and drives strategic value for the organization. So the GC absolutely has a role to play to convene all of those different stakeholders, and it requires a recognition of the multidisciplinary approach of contracting.

Be on the lookout for someone on the client side with whom you feel real chemistry, advises Steph Corey, CEO and co-founder of UpLevel Ops. It's unlikely that identifying this sense of chemistry with your prospective consensus-building partner will happen quickly (although it can). You don't want a false positive; the relationship is too important. Get to know several people on the client side until someone clicks.

> We've all worked with people who you know are great but, for whatever reason, you just didn't vibe. As a start, I think the GC and their chief of staff or head of operations really need to vibe. It's so important that they have good chemistry, because there's a trust factor there that has to develop. As the GC, I'm going to come up with that vision, and then the operations person is the one who operationalizes that vision. And I have to trust how

that person is going to get it done. I need this person to make sure that it gets done and that my team is taken care of from an operational standpoint. So I always say chemistry is first and foremost. And then you extend that relationship dynamic into the business because you're really looking for [people] who are always looking for a better way of doing things.

The chemistry between the Legal Ops leader and the client/leaders in the business has to endure, because what GenO brings to the party is not a one-off. As Corey points out, you will be working closely with your counterpart to build consensus for an ongoing process of efficiency and better outcomes.

That chemistry is so vital because you're working so hard to improve things in the department and it's never done, it's continuous improvement. You finish, let's talk about implementing a CLM. You finish, but then you're starting right over again. OK, now what can we improve? What are some other work streams we can automate? And whether you're talking about a CLM or implementing some type of new HR program in the department, you need this person, this is the change champion. So you really are looking for somebody who's a change agent, who is consensus-driven and gets people on board with things. Somebody who has that brain, there's got to be a better way to do this. Let's work to find a better way to do this. That's really what you're looking for. This applies just as much within the legal department as in any interdepartmental initiative, such as contract management.

Consensus-building is often confused with getting 100% buy-in. That's a pretty high bar, and unrealistic. In fact, it's good to have some dissenters. GenO can acknowledge their dissension and ensure that their points of view are respectfully documented. As an initiative progresses, the dissenters should be kept in the loop and if their skepticism doesn't come to fruition, then they should be presented with results in a respectful manner. It's not about proving someone wrong. It's more about moving forward with general backing of the majority of stakeholders and ensuring that stakeholders that express skepticism are still respected. Other qualities such as empathy become important here. None of the power (soft) skills and qualities are standalone—they all work together in harmony.

Co-author Prashant Dubey outlines a process designed to quantify "just the right amount of data" needed to get all parties to support an initiative.

> There is always a big looming question of "What is the ROI of a contract lifecycle management implementation?" Metrics upon metrics are gathered. Dashboards abound. Reports are created and sent around. However, what if we oversimplified it for some audiences and said, for example, "Our overarching goal is to reduce cost/contract"? A simple top-down approach can yield a target number that everyone can galvanize around, and naturally drives consensus. Here's how GenO can drive this.
>
> If 26% of people in a company touch contracts [according to World Commerce & Contracting's 2022 study "Crossing the Contract AI Chasm"], then it can't be difficult to do something like this: Quickly scan the legal department and determine how many people touch contracts. Some do it part time, some full time. Assume some high-level percentage for each person. Assume some round number for "fully loaded cost divided by FTE." Do the multiplication and get your "total cost of contracting in legal."
>
> Then get a general sense of contracts per year (plus or minus 20%) that pass through Legal, and do the division. Get your cost per contract. That's your baseline. As time goes on, monitor to see if this same team can process more contract volume by either becoming more efficient themselves, and/or by pushing some out to a "self-serve" model. (Assume it's a growth company, take the strategic plan, use the projected percentage growth in revenue and apply it linearly to the number of con-

tracts per annum.) If the answer is "yes," you have reduced your cost per contract without cutting resources, simultaneously making the Legal team happier because they're doing more substantive work. Inherent in this calculation is a faster contracting cycle time.

One number. Easy-to-make decisions. Everyone can galvanize around it. Vilfredo Pareto lives on …

Consensus-building, like rapid decision-making, is best achieved when GenO has earned the confidence of key leaders within the client units. Identify your ideal client/leaders and they will pave the way for a mutually satisfactory outcome.

Skill 12: Radical transparency—all cards face-up

Ensure that all stakeholders are kept apprised of status, whether good or bad. 'No surprises' should be GenO's commitment to its partners.

Driven by their legal department "training," many Legal Ops professionals may take a tentative approach to communicating bad news, preferring to solve challenges in the shadows rather than socializing the fact that the challenge exists. Resist this urge and embrace radical transparency.

How is this done? Ensure that all stakeholders are always kept informed, in real-time, of the status of various initiatives, including any challenges and their potential solutions. Manage Legal Ops-led initiatives with complete transparency. Ask for help in real time and ensure that stakeholders know they have a role to play in the initiative's success.

The goal is for the legal department to be viewed as being "truth tellers" who are a key resource for executives within and beyond it. And on a practical level, be upfront about technology: It may take some time to work properly; set proper expectations for it.

InnoLaw Group's Lucy Bassli explains that truth-telling is directly related to predictability—that elusive state of being that every business enabler longs for.

> When people are getting assurances that something will be done within a certain timeframe, and then that keeps not happening ... that's what creates that lack of predictability. People are adjusting their schedules and setting expectations outside their own department, and then they get the "schedule pushed back" memo. Oftentimes, all the business wants is some predictability from their law department. It's almost like not even a fight about what takes too long or not long or whatever that length is, that becomes—what is it, a symptom? The root causes, they just don't know what's going on. Nobody likes surprises. They just want predictability. So if you tell them from the beginning, "It'll take five days." "Oh, OK." They're not going to call you on Day 2 annoyed because they didn't know that that's five days.

Just as with scheduling the work that is to be done, Legal Ops needs to be truthful about how this new process will alter the current reality. GenO intuits that it is better for the client to be prepared for change—and for them to be able to discuss the ramifications for their team ahead of implementation.

Truth-telling must be based on company culture as well as the details of what is about to happen. For instance, says Cedar Cares' Tommie Tavares-Ferreira, groundwork for sharing transparently will be laid differently depending upon the company environment, the accepted norms, protocols, and need-to-knows that are unique to your client's employer.

> A lot of it is learning about your company's culture and how you navigate through it. Some companies are really cutthroat, [and] say, "I'm going directly to the C-suite" or their deputies. Then there are other companies that are flat, they're pre-IPO; some are startups; and you have complete access to the C-suite. So to navigate through who I should and can talk to, all of

those are those soft skills that are imperative. I think a huge part of our skillset [is] how do you tell the story? If you're trying to drive something, how do you express what you're trying to drive, why you're trying to drive it; how are you going to do it, and who's coming along with you? And have they all bought into why we're going on this journey together?

When you lay out a decision and someone makes the decision you're hoping they make, primarily because you've laid out a pretty viable argument and you've done your research, they get to the same place that you get to and make that decision. That's a win-win.

Rather than telling the GC, "I hear that you want to go pack the conference room with llamas"—rather than maybe doing that, [say] "Here's what I did. Here's how much the llamas cost. Here's some of the concerns that we got from the llama committees." When you lay out the facts in a transparent manner, they might go, "Maybe llamas in every conference room, it's the vibe I wanted, it's the happiness I wanted to instill culturally, but maybe we shouldn't do llamas in every conference room."

It is always better to lay out that research that you've done, and let them come to the conclusion along with you, rather than say, "Nope, no llamas in the conference rooms." Don't be the person who said, "No llamas in the conference room."

You're communicating with people about an initiative that you're essentially a facilitator; you're a steward of that initiative; and a steward of the truth of what the initiative implies, and what you believe—based on experience—the implementation will look like.

As Legal Ops has evolved, we have seen the need for radical transparency manifest in contract management initiatives where budgets get frozen and timelines for implementation get delayed. Co-author Prashant Dubey says truth-telling is vital under such conditions.

In these situations, radical transparency with all stakeholders, including the implementation team, is tantamount to organizational stability. Telling people that they may need to shift their priorities and still move the initiative forward in creative ways that don't require hard dollars, is not only transparent but respectful. Teams like to know, rather than not know, and then they have the ability to galvanize themselves and get things done ... together. It's sort of like everyone is battling a common foe. Radical transparency can often have a positive unintended consequence—bringing teams closer together.

Now that we have taken the reader through our power (soft) skills version of the CLOC wheel, we move ahead on the evolutionary track. In the next chapter, we share insights into how GenO has flourished in the relatively short time since its recognition as an enabler of efficiency and profitability across the enterprise.

8

The Evolution Continues: GenO and Generalist Counsel—Inextricably Linked

I think it's really changed over the years. There's an understanding that in-house counsel need to be part of the business. They need to be business enablers rather than business preventers, which, whether fairly or not, they're often seen as.

SALLY GUYER, *Global Chief Executive Officer,*
World Commerce & Contracting

GenO has come to represent a new generation of Legal Operations professionals going far beyond the boundaries of the law department, with a focus on the efficiency and effectiveness of the law department to being strategic business enablers in an organization. As GenO have evolved, they have become a bridge between the business, operations, and law, to the extent that Legal Ops is now its own realm within the enterprise. This has been happening for a number of years, and it's a trend that we believe will continue.

At the headwaters of this trend, the General Counsel has been viewed in organizations less as an adjudicator of risk and more as a strategic enabler to the business. Those with a legal perspective are now assumed to be problem-solvers and even revenue-generators. This trend is only going to pick up, and at an accelerated pace.

It's Interdependence, Not Codependence

As we chronicled the rise of GenO Legal Ops, it became evident to us that over the past fifteen years, the rise of the General Counsel as strategic business enabler was inextricably linked to the rise of GenO. As Mona Stone—Executive Vice President and Chief Administrative Officer of Goodwill of Central and Northern Arizona, and Chief Operating Officer and Chief Legal Officer of Thrive Services Group—said quite directly in an online course offered by the Association of Corporate Counsel, "I depend on Legal Operations for my career success."

In the 2013 book *The Generalist Counsel*, the authors charted the evolution of the General Counsel from siloed top lawyer with limited powers (and upward mobility) to the expanding role of business enabler, and called this new cadre of GCs "Generalist Counsel." The book outlined the ways in which progressive General Counsel were shifting from legal to business/legal eagles as they assumed more responsibility for business outcomes and, in so doing, began to contribute directly to the top (and bottom) line—from cost center to value creator.

But, as Goodwill's Stone and others informed us, as General Counsel they may have taken on (or been expected to take on) responsibilities beyond the traditional remit of "top lawyer." The Generalist Counsel who succeeded in this endeavor (some did, and some were unable to break out of their role as "top lawyer") were the ones who took their strategies and actually turned them into actions. As we dug further into the drivers of these GCs becoming Generalist Counsel, it was apparent to us that their Legal Operations leaders were a key driver of their success. We like to think of this as Legal Ops turning GCs' "aspirations into action."

Mark Chandler is a widely heralded Generalist Counsel. Chandler served as Chief Legal Officer and Chief Compliance Officer of Cisco Systems from 2001 to 2021, roles in which he oversaw Cisco's global legal activities and policies, as well as the ethics, regulatory compliance, and brand protection departments. Steve Harmon, whose tenure at Cisco overlapped with Chandler almost to the year, served as Vice President and Deputy General Counsel from 2000 to 2019, and built and led a Legal Operations function that, as previously described, became the training ground for many GenO Legal Operations professionals today.

In an interview of Harmon (conducted by Prashant Dubey, author and Chief Strategy Officer at Agiloft, Inc., for law company Elevate) in summer 2022, when asked about his view of the statement that a Generalist Counsel is a "businessperson who happens to be a lawyer," Harmon shared: "Mark Chandler was a tremendous mentor to me and shaped my outlook and approach to the role. Very early in my tenure at Cisco, in a global 'Law Department All Hands' meeting, he invited our head of Engineering and Products and our head of Sales to present their priorities to the Department. At the end of the presentation, someone questioned whether the time spent should focus on a specific legal topic or risk, etc. Mark replied that being an expert in our legal practice areas was table stakes for us as lawyers. Part of the reason most corporations (at least at that time in 2002) hired only from law firms was to ensure lawyers had experience and legal skills. He then observed that the corporation's ability to pay our salaries was entirely dependent on the ability of our engineers to design market-leading products and the ability of our salespeople to put those products in the hands of our customers. The law department is a tax on the business, and one of the key roles of a GC is to find a way to reduce that tax. Over time, Mark and I distilled that ethos into a mission statement for the Department: 'The mission of our Department is to enable the business to design, build, and sell its products in a legally appropriate way.' "

Harmon said that he brought that same mission statement to Elevate, where he is GC and COO, and said that mission is "our governing mission within our (Legal) Department. To deliver on that mission requires us, as lawyers, to move well beyond traditional legal advice. As we say in our Department, there are no 'legal issues'; instead, there are only business issues with legal implications." Harmon employs this same lens when executing his role as COO.

Dubey, in a subsequent conversation with Harmon, asked him if he felt that his and Chandler's success created a (productive) interdependence. Dubey contrasted this with a codependent relationship where one can "lose a part of themselves in the relationship." Harmon, always humble, said, "Well, I'm not sure if he would say that [that he and Chandler were interdependent] about me, but I sure feel that way about him. In fact, I remember when Mark gave me my annual performance reviews." Harmon said he went to Chandler's office and the meeting was all of two minutes, with Chandler saying, "Steve, you're doing great—is there anything I can do for you?" In our view that was a vote of confidence that showed trust and interdependence. In fact, our conversations with others in the Legal Operations community familiar with the Mark-Steve dynamic have almost created an aura of folklore around the relationship. Should GenO Legal Ops professionals strive to achieve such a dynamic, and is it realistic to expect it to manifest? We say yes. In fact, it's almost unavoidable, given the world today.

Not a 'Nice to Have,' but a 'Need to Have'— Quintessential Example: ESG

The current macroeconomic, regulatory, and geopolitical climate demands a more synchronized relationship between legal and operational functions. This business decision makes sense in isolation, but does it run afoul of our compliance obligations? Do things such as new sustainability reporting requirements create the need to alter our supply chain contracting processes to ensure we can comply? How does one ensure that a General Counsel chartered with stewarding Environmental, Social & Governance (ESG) initiatives (more than 53% of GCs indicated that ESG compliance was their top initiative in 2024) can, in fact, go beyond policy and ensure that ESG is built into company operations?

Contract management as an enterprise business process has become a key enabler for GenO professionals to take their rightful seat at the business strategy table. Because Legal Operations is where General Counsel aspirations are turned into action, Legal Ops become the quintessential change agents. In the context of ESG, we have observed that GenO Legal Ops and General Counsel are leveraging their interdependence to ensure that ESG doesn't start and end at proclamations but actually changes the way the company conducts business, and how it enters into contracts with customers, suppliers, and partners.

Christine Uri, founder of ESG for In-House Counsel and former Chief Legal & Sustainability Officer and General Counsel of Engie Impact, described in a presentation at the Corporate Legal Operations Consortium's 2024 CLOC Global Institute conference how law departments get involved in ESG. "ESG is about a company improving how they interact with the community around them," she says, "including their customers, suppliers, partners, and investors." In fact, she says "89% of investors consider ESG in their investment approach, 62% of buyers in an M&A transaction are willing to pay more for a company that demonstrates ESG maturity, and 67% of banks are screening loan portfolios for ESG. This all matters because companies that score high on ESG performance metrics deliver 2.6 times greater shareholder returns than companies that have medium performance. Guess what? In most companies legal is a key driver of, or participant in, ESG initiatives."

Uri describes the two scenarios in which a law department typically participates in ESG. In one scenario, the Office of General Counsel is responsible for legal issues related to ESG. "In this scenario, I often see Legal Operations as the law department delegate, participating in companywide ESG workgroups, aggregating information about legal risks related to ESG, for adjudication by the lawyers, and supporting ESG compliance reporting."

In a second scenario, the General Counsel is responsible for leading ESG companywide. Uri says, "This means the GC is setting ESG strategy, accountable for achievement of ESG objectives, and ensures the law department leads companywide ESG workgroups." She goes on to say, "Obviously it's not the GC herself that is doing these things. Ownership in this context doesn't mean doing it, but rather, ensuring it gets done." This is where GenO comes in. Turning aspirations into action is how GenO ensures that their General Counsel can achieve ESG goals on behalf of the company.

In either scenario, GenO typically engaged in things such as conducting gap assessments, tracking measurements and key performance indicators, and identifying and implementing technology. Uri describes GenO's role in the following manner: "I have seen forward-thinking Legal Ops professionals doing things such as reviewing public statements for greenwashing risk, reviewing client contracts for commitments, and supplier contracts for ESG gaps and risks. Measurements and KPIs may include things such as percent of high-risk suppliers by geography, percent completion of supplier due diligence, and contract remediation. In some companies on the leading edge, GenO will create a companywide ESG technology roadmap, implement technology to measure a company's ESG footprint, and use ESG compliance as a justification for acquiring contract lifecycle management (CLM) technology."

"It is apparent to me that this interdependence between the GC and Legal Ops will only get stronger," she says. "When I was GC at Engie Impact, I saw it firsthand when implementing a CLM program. Now that I am an adviser to General Counsel and Legal Ops on issues related to ESG, I see this dynamic manifest everyday and, frankly, it's exciting. It means that ESG programs led by GCs will, in fact, become reality because Legal Ops is where things actually get put into practice daily."

It's a Team Sport

As Legal Ops continues to be the bridge between legal, business, and technology groups in the company, we have learned that this bridge cannot sustain itself unless silos are toppled. The legal team needs to cultivate relationships with executives and other groups in the company in order to further their objective and enable the business to be more strategic. Sally Guyer, Global Chief Executive Officer for World Commerce & Contracting, watched the shift happen in real time.

Guyer recalls the pre-Legal Ops days when the in-house legal team worked heavily siloed from the rest of the business. The established way of doing things had become a breeding ground for inefficiency. The disconnect between the legal department and the rest of the business was glaring and apparent.

> In the early days of my career, the in-house counsel and in-house legal teams still took the approach that they needed to be at arm's length from other departments. Almost like an internal external counsel. It was always very confusing. We heard in the past so often that the legal teams are sitting in their ivory tower, distant and disconnected. I think that that was a reality in many instances, not across the board, but generally it was quite a reality. But that's really changed over recent years. There's an understanding that in-house counsel really need to be part of the business. They need to be business enablers rather than business preventers.

Our observation is that this same dynamic-shift is occurring with the Legal Ops community. Perhaps when implementing an e-billing system, much of the discourse can be intralegal (of course Finance needs to be involved). However, when thinking about legal knowledge management, company strategies around data "marts/lakes/warehouses/lake-houses" and AI large language models need to be considered. These conversations involve IT, digital transformation, cross-functional teams, and executive management. Similarly, enterprise contract management is just that—an enterprise initiative. Yes, legal has a role to play but the entire company interacts with contracts. We have already talked in detail about ESG, vendor compliance, and other initiatives that necessitate interactions with departments and people outside of Legal.

From 'Just Do It' to Mr. Commodore

Lizzie Shilliam, Chief of Staff and Legal Operations, Office of the General Counsel at Vanderbilt University, described the dynamic the following way: "When I initially looked at our contract management processes, I realized that we needed better technology to automate our manual processes, track obligations, and give university departmental leadership visibility into all these things. I started with making the case that being forced to use the contract management module of our ERP [enterprise resource planning] system would not allow me to accomplish these goals. So, I set off on a quest to learn in detail the contracting needs and pains, universitywide, department by department, and then used this information to convince our chancellor that a specialized enterprise contracting platform is necessary for an institution like ours. This required me to step outside of the law department and truly view contracting as an enterprise business process and make a business case with confidence that represented a university-wide lens."

Shilliam broke down silos at Nike, Hertz, and now Vanderbilt University—proof that silos are not limited to any particular industry or size of organization. Legal Ops is a team sport.

Back to School—in the Battlegrounds

Sally Guyer likes to say, "The modules that are taught at law school are all about things that go wrong. Lawyers in training are naturally conditioned as students to think about the things that go wrong, and to assume that their role is to protect bad things from happening to the organization." The emergence of GenO represents a radical departure from this mindset—a mindset that, for the most part, is not even discussed in most law schools, where "protect and defend" is still the philosophical bedrock.

For those students who are seeking a law degree or legal training to (eventually) work for a company, most law schools offer little or no preparation for a career outside the law department. Yet in the real world, GenO professionals are coming to the law department from finance, procurement, strategy, IT, and operations, getting their skills honed, then being placed in value-creation groups/teams such as strategic alliances, digital transformation, and revenue optimization. If a lawyer gets their start in the law department, often, if they embrace their remit as a "businessperson who happens to be a lawyer," they are being dispersed throughout the enterprise in these same value-creation groups. Why? Because their value in terms of optimizing revenue, profit, and risk is being recognized.

This isn't to say that being able to defend intellectual property or contractual rights is not part of the role; of course it is. But it misses the fundamental piece of being a business enabler; for example, enabling successful outcomes from the contracts that the business enters into. By taking positive action upstream in the contracting process, the need to defend is reduced. Legal Ops performs this service by streamlining contract process and flow (referred to by analysts as "orchestration"), anticipating where difficulties can arise, and proactively reducing the likelihood of legal entanglements.

GenO, in their desire to take on the role of strategic business partner, is making this mindset shift in real time, on the job. This revolutionary way of practicing law in the corporate setting is driven by a rising number of Legal Ops practitioners and such organizations as the Corporate Legal Operations Consortium (CLOC). The legal education for this emerging generation, which might be expected to happen in law school, is thus actually taking place within the enterprise, as well as at conferences, seminars, and corporate retreats. What we are seeing from the 10,000-foot view is an energized, integrated Legal Ops community with much greater optimism about its role in the delivery of successful outcomes. Where law schools have just started recognizing their role in this community, the industry at large is an active learning ground for GenO professionals.

Intel Corporation's head of Global Legal Operations, Mike Haven, during an "UpLevel View" podcast in July 2024, spoke to Steph Corey, CEO and Co-Founder of UpLevel Ops, as well as to Jenn McCarron, President of the Corporate Legal Operations Consortium, about how collaboration born from necessity is what caused Legal Ops to even become a profession. McCarron, Haven, and Corey all described how CLOC started out as a book club in 2015 then became almost a "support group" of sorts for Legal Ops professionals, many of whom were the only ones in their company performing their role. They talked about how they looked within their companies for support and found few that understood the Legal Ops remit. When they looked across the industry at other companies, they found camaraderie with others similarly situated. What started out as a "birds of a feather" support group blossomed into a global organization of thousands of like-minded professionals who freely collaborated, shared best-practices, and helped each other navigate the ambiguity of a newly defined profession. Law schools and other formal teaching institutions did not provide such support. Nature abhors a void, and the industry came together to fill it.

Breaking the Glass Injunction

Before we make the detailed case for the rise of GenO as organizational leader, let's address the big question: Can an outstanding Legal Operations professional aspire to be a C-suite executive? This may seem like a stretch at this point. But remember, when *The Generalist Counsel* was published in 2013, there was some skepticism that the road to the corner office could run through Legal. Since then, countless GCs have been appointed CEO, including Jeff Kindler (Pfizer), Ken Frazier (Merck), Lloyd Blankfein (Goldman Sachs), and Horace Dawson (Red Lobster).

As noted in Chapter 8 of *The Generalist Counsel*, "a fully formed Generalist Counsel has as much right to aspire to be CEO as any other senior executive, but simply having been a General Counsel does not qualify anyone to be Chief Executive. And, while we also agree that the ascendancy from General Counsel to the CEO position is not something new, we do believe there are factors at play in business today that may create the perfect environment for General Counsel to move into CEO roles with increasing frequency. ... As we have discovered, and as validated by our storytellers, there is no 'playbook' for making the transition from General Counsel to CEO and every situation is different."[1]

We believe the same is now true for GenO Legal Ops professionals. Many start with operational skills such as finance, vendor management, contract negotiation, IT, and project/program management; then, as they ascend and broaden their remit, they add the soft/power skills outlined in Chapters 6 and 7. This, combined with the right experience, mentoring, some "right place, right time" executive exposure, and—let's be frank—ambition, indicates that the glass injunction between Legal Ops and the C-suite is waiting to be overturned.

Far-fetched? We don't think so.

Follow the Yellow Brick Roads

The position of General Counsel requires a law degree, so for someone without that degree, the path beyond legal would, in theory, not go through GC. But what is the general direction of travel?

---
1. Prashant Dubey and Eva Kripalani, *The Generalist Counsel: How Leading General Counsel Are Shaping Tomorrow's Companies* (New York: Oxford University Press, 2013), 137.

If Legal Ops becomes its own department/discipline within Legal, then the Chief of Legal Ops or the COO of Legal titles are certainly a possibility. That opens the way to C-suite interactions, often as a surrogate for the GC. We are seeing this becoming more of a trend, especially in complex enterprises. Bob Mignanelli is an example of this. As Vice President of Legal Strategy/Operations, Digital & Technology, and Procurement at Haleon, he has been the GC's right hand for many years. Yes, he is a lawyer, but it's his business acumen that has allowed him such a broad remit. Can he sit at the table with any C-suite executive and discuss business issues that impact the company and identify value-creation opportunities? Not only can he, but he does, on a daily basis.

It was 2014, when Mignanelli first met Bjarne Tellmann. Mignanelli had been at educational publisher Pearson for about 13 years at the time, and Tellman had just joined Pearson. When they had their first meeting, Mignanelli felt Tellman was the kind of person who would appreciate initiative and proactive ideas. So, Mignanelli took a leap of faith. Essentially he said, "Bjarne, there's nothing that crosses my desk here that I can't handle. I've seen it before. I want a new challenge." Bold? Certainly. Well-earned and deserved? Of course. A month later, Tellman had Mignanelli take over legal support for a critical part of the Pearson business: strategic alliances. When Tellman moved over to GSK Consumer Health (now Haleon), Mignanelli followed. Over the years, when speaking about Mignanelli, Tellman's recurring theme has been that "Bob truly is a business leader, and he simply gets things done." The successes of the GC and Legal Ops are inextricably linked and the Mignanelli/Tellman relationship is a prime example of this. Incidentally, the fact that Mignanelli is a lawyer is a side note; it helps him execute his remit but as he has said, "It's that I can sit beside my colleagues in the business and discuss business issues as a peer, not just be viewed as someone who adjudicates legal risk."

Growth and career opportunities outside the legal department may depend on the industry. Procurement leadership is an obvious option for many industries. Indirect procurement is industry-agnostic, and Legal Ops often interacts with Procurement in domains such as implementing CLM systems, so a transition is natural. Companies reliant on government contracts might value promoting a Legal Ops staff member familiar with public sector contracting to marketing, sales, logistics—potential steppingstones to the top. Companies with major distribution operations would value Legal Ops experience in various positions that require analytic and project management skills. Tech companies with a large intellectual property presence would be another place for upward mobility, leveraging Legal Ops familiarity with serving IP lawyers with technology and processes.

We have seen Legal Ops professionals in industries such as insurance transition to strategic planning positions. Lindsey Klemyk is just such a professional. Klemyk built the Legal Ops function at Aetna, supported the acquisition of Aetna by CVS, and rolled out a major contract management initiative amid all this change. After nineteen impactful years at Aetna, Klemyk joined MassMutual and is, as of this writing, Head of Planning, Portfolio Management and Analytics for the Enterprise Technology & Experience (ETX) organization. Is she on the path to senior leadership? We say yes.

Advancement will be driven by a focus on business processes combining risk, cost, technology, and human participation. The risk element is what drives the need for the legal background, as well. In many ways, the conditions for GenO's rise mirror those that led to the emergence of General Counsel as CEO material.

Mindset Reset

In *The Generalist Counsel*, Jeff Kindler—who then was senior adviser at Paragon Pharmaceuticals and now is CEO at Centrexion Therapeutics Corporation—described the shift in mindset that needs to occur for a lawyer to break out of the law department. Kindler served as the top lawyer at General Electric Co. and

McDonald's Corporation before becoming president of McDonald's Brands and, eventually, General Counsel and then Chairman and CEO of Pfizer, Inc.

Kindler noted that legal training dictates there is a right answer for every question posed to the lawyer; "solving" a problem is simply a matter of digging until the answer is found.

"In business," he said, "it is quite different, especially either in the early stages of entrepreneurial operations or the later stages of very mature organizations. There simply are no clear answers to profound questions. As a business leader, I'm not looking for a right answer but the best decision based upon the circumstances.

"The second thing is operating experience. There is not any substitute for operating and profit and loss experience. The difference is huge between being an adviser and being the person who has the ultimate responsibility for P&L and general management. Anyone who is aspiring to be a business leader should try to acquire that P&L."

Kindler's guidance was for General Counsel who aspired to be CEO. However, we posit that with GenO we are starting to see the beginnings of a similar evolution of Legal Ops careers. Call it toxic positivity. Guilty as charged.

Take—or Make—Opportunities for Growth

Kindler's career trajectory was, in its day, nontraditional. But the route charted by Home Depot's Frank Blake from General Counsel to CEO, as chronicled in *The Generalist Counsel*, was off-the-charts unusual.[2] Blake's case serves as perhaps an extreme example of opportunistic career advancement. But the lesson is clear: Create, don't wait.

Blake came straight up the public-sector legal ladder. His early gigs included clerking for U.S. Supreme Court Justice John Paul

---

2. Prashant Dubey and Eva Kripalani, *The Generalist Counsel: How Leading General Counsel Are Shaping Tomorrow's Companies* (New York: Oxford University Press, 2013), 147.

Stevens and serving as Vice President George W. Bush's deputy counsel. Then he went to the private sector, landing as General Counsel for GE Power Systems. A true whirlwind of a career by most standards, it turned out he was just getting started.

At GE he crossed over to the business side. As vice president of Power Systems' business development, he demonstrated that he was not bound to his law books. After a stint as a senior VP at GE, he bounced back to the public sector as deputy secretary with the U.S. Department of Energy. Then he made his most critical move: Executive VP of Business Development at Home Depot. Soon, he was running the company, much to the dismay of others who lusted after the CEO position there.

As recounted in *The Generalist Counsel*: "Leaving a position of corporate clout at GE to return to the public sector, where he had already served several times, might seem incongruous to an executive seeking power and a healthy compensation package, but Blake has used his combination of legal expertise and corporate experience to satisfy his proclivity for testing his abilities in new forums. He constantly sought out roles to hone his business chops and gain experiences that would allow him to be 'business accountable.'

"When Blake was tapped to run Home Depot in 2002, the selection confounded retail industry experts, given his lack of retail experience. He replaced Bob Nardelli, known for his aggressive and, many say, abrasive style.

"By all accounts, Blake has handled controversy and corporate restructuring with aplomb, inspiring one admirer to dub him 'calmer-in-chief.' Blake … has generally overseen tough calls with a tolerant, humble style that has won him the admiration of many Home Depot employees and customers. When someone suggests that lawyers are a bit lacking in the empathy department, you may wish to respond with a suggestion that they read up on calmer-in-chief, Frank Blake."

Why are we retelling these stories of the General Counsel's ascension to CEO? What does this have to do with Legal

Ops? A lot. Twenty years ago, a few posited that GCs were perfectly positioned to lead companies. They were laughed out of the room as heretics and idealistic or, worst-case, motivated by misplaced ambition. Similarly, Mary Barra, Chairman and CEO of General Motors, was not swayed by critics when at 18 years of age she worked on the assembly line at GM, inspecting hoods and fenders.

Our optimism has a basis in fact. If we are still fortunate enough to have a place on this earth in fifteen years, we are confident vindication is forthcoming.

Contracts Are Data—but Also Relationships

Today's GenO rising stars, like the General Counsel pioneers profiled in *The Generalist Counsel*, are charting various routes up Corporate Mount Everest. But most of them share a common point of origin: the management of data found in legal documents; in a word, contracts.

Contracts are first and foremost economic instruments. But who "owns" these contracts? Is it the law department, where they are, if not birthed, at least christened and sanctified? Or do the business divisions claim ownership, since they are the ones that generate the need for the documents? In reality, as instruments that dictate the health and wealth of an organization, they are the property of both.

But it is Legal Ops that takes true ownership of the fate of these documents, and extracts their full value on behalf of the enterprise. From humble beginnings—the storage of documents so they could be produced on demand—Legal Ops has become the master of contract data management across the enterprise. It now claims the active management of the documents that underlie virtually every business transaction. And that is where GenO's potential to penetrate the C-suite lies. World Commerce & Contracting's Sally Guyer elucidates:

Contracts can be used as operational guides to drive the successful outcomes that we aspire to in the first place, that have driven us to put the contract in place in the first place. Recognize that contracts and the contracting process is multidisciplinary, then we need to make sure that we are designing that process and the documents, the instruments themselves, for the user community.

Understanding that a contract can be the basis of a relationship rather than just a transaction is key to GenO's upward mobility. As Guyer notes, a document roadmap—from creation to execution—will reveal who needs to be involved in this "corporate-wide" initiative.

It's about developing relationships, and getting a grasp of what your contracting process looks like in your organization; which organizations and teams are involved in contracting. Once you've identified the teams, departments, and business units that are involved in the process, start developing the relationship. Start listening to them, start understanding what their pain points are, what works well, what doesn't work well. The GC absolutely has a role to play to convene all of those different stakeholders, and it requires a recognition of the multidisciplinary approach of contracting.

It's a multidisciplinary process, one that gives GenO visibility across the organization. The legal team must also do its share of self-education as they enter into this new dynamic. By developing productive relationships with their peers at other corporations, they can share experiences that will further their own agenda of taking their rightful seat at a business strategy table. CLOC provides such a learning environment. And for those looking for growth opportunities, peer relationships can open doors more quickly than might be the case with a current employer.

The forward-thinking Legal Operations professional will want to be the instigator and orchestrator of this relationship initiative. Until the day arrives when Legal Ops is accepted as a proving ground for more elevated responsibilities, GenO leaders must be tireless advocates for professional advancement.

Starting Legal Ops from Scratch

The adoption of Legal Operations by the enterprise has become so widespread that we sometimes forget how quickly that evolution has taken place. But to understand where GenO is headed, it is instructive to examine its roots. Vanderbilt University's Lizzie Shilliam played a critical role in building Legal Ops departments at Nike and Hertz in the second decade of the current millennium. Her work establishing Legal Operations at these two goliaths of industry helped pave the way for those who followed.

Soon after she joined Nike in 2009, she took on the task of reorganizing its contract management process.

> I had brought up to our CFO that we had risk in not knowing where all of our contracts were. I was in the procurement team at that time and we couldn't find contracts. They were in drawers, people had saved them to their hard drives, they were in all sorts of places, and that was a hot-potato risk for quite a while. It got passed around to quite a few different departments, and finally he called me into his office one day and said, "Well, you started this mess, let's clean it up." And so he gave me a large budget and he also gave me headcount to hire and consultants to hire to figure out contract management at Nike and put a global solution in place.
>
> The risk was identified to the board of trustees, so that was done at the top level. But more importantly, we had to knock on doors because just because the board of trustees said to do it, it doesn't always mean that everybody participates. So we went door to door talking to directors, talking to senior directors, asking them where their contracts were. We found some very funny things. There was one story of a lady that had the contracts secured, and I asked where they were and she said, "They're in the box in the back of my car, and at least I always have them with me."

> Pretty soon we realized that if we were going to look at all of these contracts and put a system in place, number one, we had to find all of the contracts per department. That was a huge project. But the second one was we had to extract the metadata from those contracts to make it useful in the system itself.
>
> So we put together a team of attorneys that had decided they didn't want to practice the traditional path of law, and they were a fantastic group.

Thus did Shilliam create the first GenO class at Nike. They had no playbook for advancement. They just knew they wanted to be part of something new and exciting, and trusted that Shilliam would lead them to wherever it was they were bound.

Putting Hertz in the Driver's Seat

Shilliam then moved on to Hertz, again tasked with implementing the Legal Ops concept. There, she had an ally in place: Tom Sabatino, the General Counsel at Hertz. Sabatino was among those profiled in *The Generalist Counsel*. Himself a pioneer at moving beyond the confines of the law department, Sabatino doubtless recognized a kindred revolutionary spirit in Shilliam. With her star hitched to his, her ascension was inevitable.

> Tom was a fantastic General Counsel, quite the visionary. And we had a lot of conversations about how we were going to do this. We came up with a strategic plan that was about three years long, and we started talking to the rest of the legal department about what they could do in each of their areas to improve service to the organization.
>
> And one of those things was that we did not have information from our invoices from outside counsel, that because they were charged back to the individual teams, they didn't really have visibility into that and why they were being charged. They just knew it would hit their bottom line and they would have to pay the bills. So we started giving them transparency into what was being charged to outside counsel, why it was being

charged, and how that impacted their budget in a more transparent way, that they could then see what was happening with their matters.

And when that started, then we started building a lot of trust with the business owners. And so when we went to the contract management implementation, it was much easier because we could actually talk to them about why we needed to track contracts and how we needed to put the metadata into the system and how that might look long-term. So it's really that relationship-building, the change-management time that you put into it, and the executive support that helps drive successful completion of those projects.

Shilliam and Sabatino were speaking the language of the business enablers. No longer viewed as risk managers, naysayers, and law journal aficionados, they bridged the gap between legal and business—and opened up new vistas of career opportunities for themselves and their acolytes.

Full Partnership in Business Outcomes

In many organizations, Legal Operations has embedded itself so thoroughly throughout the enterprise that it is hard now to imagine how business got done before its advent. With a cohort of experienced GenO professionals now in place, the evolution of the role will certainly continue unabated. Connie Brenton, Founder and CEO of LegalOps.com, offers her perspective as a witness to, and key participant in, that evolution.

The role of the Legal Operations professional has been in parallel with the evolution of the role of the General Counsel. Back then, the General Counsel was a figurehead. It was somebody who didn't have the wherewithal to make it in private practice, so they'd put them in there and they would manage outside counsel. We are a far cry from that now. Now General Counsel are considered business partners. Many General Counsel are moving into strategy roles and CEO roles. And with that comes the evolution of the Legal Operations role. In essence, and this is with legalops.com, we are redefining, again, the role of the Legal Operations executive as fifteen practice areas. But the practice areas in reality are the job of the General Counsel, and they are simply delegating it just like they would delegate commercial sales or employment or privacy. It has become a practice area of its own as the role and as the evolution of the General Counsel continue to move.

The opportunities for GenO to prove its worth seem limitless. Consider the pandemic-driven explosion of remote and contract employees replacing office-bound workers. While disruptive initially, corporations are adjusting, and are discovering potential cost-saving offsets in the bargain. But this cannot be accomplished effectively or profitably without GenO's unique expertise.

On the employee level, the shift calls for new contractual arrangements between labor and management. Who will manage this trick without the support of Legal Operations? Or consider the physical aspects of a remote workforce: Office leases must be renegotiated; buildings and properties sold; new facilities leased or acquired. It will be the responsibility of Legal Operations to ensure that there is a process and systems to ensure these transactions go smoothly, and that any new agreements take into account the possibility of some new form of pandemic that further disrupts the way work is done.

These and other looming challenges that will ultimately be described and codified in contracts of one type or another will demand an ever greater presence of the GenO professional within the enterprise—including at the leadership level. As GenO increases its understanding of the business itself, its ability to better serve the whole will expand exponentially. Astute corporate leaders are already recognizing the breadth of knowledge Legal Ops' rising stars have acquired, promoting them to key positions where legal expertise, relationship-building, and business outcomes are valued.

Legal Training as CEO Requirement?

An observation from *The Generalist Counsel* concerning the rise of the General Counsel seems apropos here. P.D. Villarreal, who then was Senior Vice President of Global Litigation for GlaxoSmithKline and now is a partner at Gilbert Litigators & Counselors, was discussing the likelihood that the role of General Counsel would soon be seen as an excellent training ground for future CEOs.

"Though Villarreal insists he has no CEO aspirations, he says this: 'It seems to hit a General Counsel at some point in their career that there's one more step they'd like to take. Companies have increasingly come to understand that so much of what they do has a legal aspect to it. As a result, the influence of the General Counsel has grown.'

" 'We have talked for a long time about how lawyers need to learn more about business,' he adds. 'But we may have reached the phase where that's no longer the case. Now, perhaps the business people need to learn about the law rather than the lawyers needing to learn about the business.' "[3]

That sounds like GenO, does it not? Yes, the future shines brightly for GenO. However, the past has not been without its missteps, and there will be some bumps in the road ahead. The GenO professional would do well to consider the painful lessons of the Legal Ops pioneers before charging too swiftly ahead.

---

3. Prashant Dubey and Eva Kripalani, *The Generalist Counsel: How Leading General Counsel Are Shaping Tomorrow's Companies* (New York: Oxford University Press, 2013), 151.

9

Cautionary Tales

I was asked once, 'What's the best professional advice you've received?' So, I'd like to give a tribute to my mom, 'Mama Shen,' who's given me some great life lessons. Lesson 1: Do it right the first time with very little questions. Lesson 2: Dress for the job you want, not the job you have. Lesson 3: If you have to be asked, it's too late. Lesson 4: Fast is always better than slow ... and slow is useless.

MARY (SHEN) O'CARROLL, *Chief Operating Officer, Goodwin*

We can safely say that the Legal Ops community would not be what it is without Mary O'Carroll. Not only was she a co-founder of the Corporate Legal Operations Consortium (CLOC), but her constant advocacy for—and guidance to—the community has provided immeasurable value to all of us. Her time at Google set many standards for Legal Ops daily practice. The advice O'Carroll gives us above may sound simple, but it is clarity that is hard-earned through years of trial and error, successes, and, yes, likely some failures. Mama Shen's sage advice, delivered through her daughter, is poignant in its simplicity.

As such, through our interviews we have learned that all may not be all rosy on the pathway to becoming a strategic business enabler. Wrong turns may be taken (though they often are seen in the rearview mirror as one's true path). Careers have been derailed (and set back on a new rail). In this chapter we will cover the importance of patience as well as experimentation. We'll talk about how it's important to know if something is not feeling right and to stop doing it. Even seasoned legal professionals have their tall tales to tell from their years in the industry. Keep, start, stop exercises are not just for the newly minted.

Our interviewees universally felt that often their faulty decision-making was a result of not cultivating their General Counsel to recognize the same problems they saw. One of the notable exceptions to this is Lizzie Shilliam, currently head of Legal Operations at Vanderbilt University, who spent the requisite time to educate Tom Sabatino on the "state of the state" when she joined Hertz.

As explained by Sabatino—one of the most experienced General Counsel on any continent, who empowered both the General Counsel's office and Legal Operations—systems and processes are the lifeblood for success in a company. A lack of these systems is like a blocked artery: It does nothing but slow down the momentum that you and your team have built. The alert GenO (in this case, Shilliam) sees the gap and sets about to build the necessary steps to smoother flow.

> When you don't have the right systems in place, the amount of friction that it causes in the organization and the amount of lost opportunity and revenue is something people don't focus a lot on. I've come to companies where we didn't have good systems. The amount of effort and time that everybody has to take—from the lawyers to the finance people to the business people—slows the organization down. That's the risk you run when you don't spend the money, don't spend the effort, don't recognize the opportunity cost to not get this thing moving.

This wasn't just Sabatino being prescient. Yes, Hertz was far from his first rodeo. However, would he have been able to articulate the issues with core systems and the need to properly resource the problem, so fluidly without a proper education from his Legal Ops leader? Likely not.

So, what's the caution? Go visit the Wizard. Ensure she is educated on the problem space. Not doing so leaves one on an island without the requisite support. Sometimes a cautionary tale can be related by talking about a success and wondering what it would have been like if the work wasn't done to create the success.

You Will Trip—Keep Your Head Up, Knees Up, and Keep Moving

The natural ebbs and flows of a business can seem disheartening at times. Sabatino's experience shines a light on perseverance, and intrapreneurial thinking—the holy quest for the best way to do things.

> You'll go through some challenging times. I've been at several companies when there were tough times. It's hard. Especially when you're told the budget's cut, we're not going to increase your staff, but we need you to do more. It's a tough message, but you have to learn how to spin things to where it's more of an opportunity. Forcing yourself and your team to think critically in that moment can be the beacon of light you need to get you through a tough spot.

> There's tons of risk in the enterprise, and you're constantly getting hit from all angles. Have your head on a swivel, with an understanding of how your role contributes to the objectives of not only the law department, but of the enterprise.

Gerald Wright faced this situation when he was at Intel Corporation. Intel as a company is subject to macroeconomic and geopolitical shifts more than most. In late 2022, Wright faced this situation and his budget was frozen. This was a critical time. Wright and his team were in the middle of a business-critical contract lifecycle management system implementation that required external resources to kick off the process. No longer did he have funding to continue to engage these external resources. What did he do?

First, Wright met with his team and was transparent. He didn't hide the ball.

> I got my team together and told them what I know. I told them we had no money to spend and would have to stop engaging the external party. I gave them a few days to absorb this and scheduled a meeting for us to get together a few days later and brainstorm about what to do.

It is notable that not only did Wright tell his team the exact situation, right when he knew, but he gave them ownership of the problem *and* the solution. Turning lemons into lemonade? He sure did.

'Grinding It Out' Is Often Overlooked As a Strategy

Getting bottom-line results is the goal, but not at any cost. One must resist the urge to charge in on one's white horse to save the enterprise from itself. Too often in the early days of Legal Ops, practitioners saw their role as crusaders rather than measured change agents. That led to interdepartmental clashes, strained relationships, and time lost to repairing the damage. It's also important to understand that, while you seek a collaborative approach to systems change, Legal Ops still takes responsibility for outcomes—including the failed ones. So sometimes it's just patience, perseverance, and seeing where the light doesn't shine its brightest.

Wright's view of Legal Ops in its early days is that it was somewhat nightmarish. Few within the enterprise understood its objectives, its practices, its applications. Cooperation was not easily forthcoming; nor was support from the C-suite in many cases. The independent nature of a fresh Legal Operations position made it easier for him to figure out business problems on his own and take the responsibility for the outcomes. But he was navigating a minefield as a pioneering GenO professional, and he had to push ahead knowing there would be blowback down the road.

> There were very small pieces of the business that Legal Operations handled. Back then, the organizations were not supporting that kind of work I did. I would tell them, "We can be much more efficient if we do it this way," but they didn't see value. They didn't see the savings, the results to the bottom line. But we said at Intel, "You own your own employment." I took that to heart. I pushed ahead anyway, because I knew it was the right thing.

This notion of personal independence, and personal responsibility, in the Legal Ops department fosters a leadership mentality within the department. Outside it, those qualities will win the trust a company has for Legal Ops. With persistence, patience, transparency, and good intentions, efficiencies can be obtained that save a company time and money—even if the results are not understood immediately.

Wright, former leader of the Global Contract Solutions Group at Intel and currently retired, is not alone among our interviewees who had the unhappy experience of successfully executing a plan and receiving complaints rather than the expected accolades. It was not in his nature to be discouraged by such a response.

> Leadership says, "Maybe I don't see the need for that." At their level, that was their thought. But at my level, what I've been doing in my career at the company, I've seen the inefficiencies. I said, "Well, I think we do need it." The process of putting an agreement in place was painful, because every legal professional, every lawyer, had their own bag of tricks. In reality, the inefficiencies caused by differences between each lawyer's practice was not seen by them. So I just pushed on.

That initiative that no one else saw the need for? Standardizing how nondisclosure agreements (NDAs) were created and negotiated and approved and executed. "It's an amazing program today," he reports. "We've driven so much efficiency [that] it takes probably five to ten minutes to get an NDA signed now. When I started, it was ten to fifteen days." Wright would just "grind it out," and not show his frustrations. That's not easy.

Wright advises a dualistic approach to establishing the continuous improvement mission of Legal Ops within legal and across other departments: Understand that you will establish an agreed-upon pacing and expected outcome as your team works with your client. That's the current playbook. Stick to the playbook. But don't be afraid to create new methods to approach new levels of efficiency. This is where there may be some pain involved. The savvy GenO professional knows how to keep their head above water, with their eyes on the prize. A cautionary tale, in retrospect, becomes a new playbook win.

Know Who You Are

Some of us knew from an early age exactly what we wanted to do when we grew up. For the rest of us, the search for a true calling can be elusive. Until recently, a career in Legal Ops was not something young lawyers (or legal minds) aspired to. Most of those interviewed for this book found their way to a GenO career after a series of false starts. Another quality they have in common is knowing when they were *not* in the right position, and taking action to extricate themselves. The lesson here isn't don't fail in a job, but don't fail to extricate yourself from it if it's not the right fit.

Connie Brenton, Founder and CEO of LegalOps.com, felt the tug of a career in law early on. But first, she had to satisfy other interests.

> When you're starting a career, part of the necessary journey is to figure out what you do not like. From the age of 5, I knew I would be an attorney, so it was a natural progression, although it may not look like it on a résumé. I am a serial entrepreneur.

> I have had a gift store in Colorado for thirty years, I've started a care package business, and I've started a bar and restaurant. Part of the journey really has been understanding and identifying and changing what I do not like to do.
>
> My first direct venture into law was as a litigator in the personal injury space, but it wasn't a great fit for me. I did it for many, many years. I have a very strong empathy gene in my soul, so it was so hard for me to separate the emotion from the work. Over time, it got to be exhausting and not fun any longer. It was at that point that I thought, "I love business."

Play to Your Strengths

With her eyes set in the business sector, Brenton got a job at Storage Tech. But her expectations of the position were quickly dashed.

> The first week they handed me just a load of agreements. I thought, "Oh my God, what was I thinking? They hired me because I'm a lawyer." Every day I remember all of that suffering we went through doing deals and signing contracts from a process perspective. That's when I realized the potential for contributing. I realized, that's what my goal is: to solve that for the company—not just the legal department, but for the business. The goal is to have the most accurate, efficient contracts system for the company that we've ever had in our history.

So Brenton redefined the objectives for her role midflight and took the initiative to put a contracting system in place that delivered results. That's not what she was hired to do, but she did it anyway. She played to her strengths, and it helped her and her company. Then she stopped doing the job—she had done what needed to be done.

> Often, you figure out what the role is after you've taken the role. Then you go through another set of experiences: Is this

something that I love? Is this something that I'm great at doing? And as you get more mature in your career, it's easier to stay in your sweet spot. There's a whole series of studies that says, play to your strengths. Don't spend all this time trying to get better at what you're not inherently good at. And if you do that and it kind of comes and goes during the career path, if you love what you're doing, keep doing that. If something changes, get out.

Sometimes you have to have experiences that you don't enjoy in order to know what you do enjoy. In contrast, it's a lot easier to identify the things you enjoy. If you can look back at something and say, "I don't want to do that. I don't like the characteristics of that experience," that allows you to gravitate towards things you are passionate about.

Brenton's emphasis on experiences and their formative nature allows Legal Ops professionals to craft the future they feel they will best excel in.

If young Legal Operations professionals are starting off in their career and they're saying, "I'm suffering. I really don't like this," take lessons from it and say, "What don't you like?" Shape what you want to do from the experiences. There's learning everywhere. Everything that you are doing in your career is somehow relevant at another point in your career, whether you liked doing it or whether you didn't like doing it.

Today, Brenton is a GenO leader who has found her niche. She didn't get there without a few wrong turns that proved to be learning opportunities. And she will tell you Legal Ops isn't for everyone. Relationship-building, tech mastery, constantly revising the playbook, and a likelihood of job-hopping can be stressful as well as fulfilling. Know your tolerance for gaining a foothold in an evolving field, and know when it isn't fun anymore.

Managing a Legal Ops Playbook … or Is It Playbooks?

Tommie Tavares-Ferreira, who runs the Legal Operations function at Cedar Cares, Inc., explains that making assumptions that solutions that worked in one environment will work in the next can lead to painful situations. She likes the idea of a Legal Ops playbook. But the playbook should not be considered applicable for all circumstances. Attempting to force the solution that worked for your previous employer onto your new one can lead to a quick loss of confidence in your ability to get the job done. Tavares-Ferreira initially took the approach of leveraging "what she knew," but then quickly realized Cedar was a different business with a different history and different personalities. She needed a new playbook, borne from experience but still built for the new environment. The agile GenO understands that knowing the business and its unique culture can put you in front of your company with solutions and positive outcomes.

> No matter what you do, even if you do have a playbook, you have to accept that you will deviate from it. Know the business, know what's happening. You want to approach it from a business-centric sense of: How am I solving our specific problems? It's that soft skill of listening, of hearing what people actually need and what they don't need.

Lucy Bassli, founder and principal of InnoLaw Group, PLLC, offers valuable insight into the convoluted nature of the Legal Operations role—insight hard-won through her own trials as a GenO pioneer. Her playbook was written by trial and error as much as by wins and losses.

> A concept I learned from one of my buddies who's a management consulting professional: "We make order out of chaos." The platform that I was given was a messy business process. When I came into the legal department, it was perceived as a

black hole, a blocker. I said, "Well, I can't have that," and that was it. I was given this opportunity, but it wasn't handed to me as an opportunity—it was a problem that needed solving. I turned it into an opportunity, through trial and error, and many times without being sanctioned from above. It wasn't always comfortable, but I knew what had to be done. And there remains great change to be made in the role.

Playbooks are important. A recognition that the need to be built for each unique situation and business is even more important.

Credentialing Can Become a Curse … If You Let It

James Donald is General Counsel, Regional Support and Legal Operations at hospitality company Accor. In other words, he is highly accomplished. He is a legal and business executive at one of the largest and most profitable hotel groups in the world. Prior to Accor, Donald was a senior legal executive at International Hotels Group, an associate at Reed Smith, and obtained his law degree from the widely heralded Northumbria University. In other words, he's highly accomplished and highly credentialed.

Accor has more than 5,500 hotels in its group with more than 800,000 rooms. There are 1,300 more hotels in the pipeline with more than 100,000 rooms. Outside of the continental United States (where Hilton and Marriott are the largest hotel groups), Accor is the largest. So it's big and iconic. Most of the largest hotel groups are "asset light," which means they don't directly own the hotels but run management and franchise contracts on behalf of third-party owners. Donald describes the business fundamentals in the following manner:

> Ultimately, we sign a deal where we have long-term contracts for ten to twenty years in some cases, and Accor takes a percentage of revenue and a percentage of profit as well … if it's a managed agreement. So contracts are basically how we run

our organization. It's a very high-margin business. It's a really interesting business. It throws off a lot of free cash. It's very generally safe.

This means that contracts are the lifeblood of Accor and a bad contracting process fraught with risk and inefficiency can become almost existential. Why does this matter? Accor was facing a situation that is similar to more than 90% of companies today. They had thousands of executed contracts sitting in shared drives, hard drives, and, yes, even paper in locations all over the globe. There were hundreds of contractual elements that needed to be managed to ensure that properties in the portfolio were managed in a way that ensures the Accor guest experience is exemplary. The company was growing rapidly and the risk of missing obligations or not tracking obligations franchisees had to Accor was getting higher daily.

So when Donald joined the company in 2019, he created a Legal Operations function and the company made a decision to implement a contract lifecycle management (CLM) platform. At some level, this was an easy decision. As Donald stated:

> We had to have a very close working relationship with our owners that's governed by the framework of our agreements, and consequently what we needed to have was good data and knowledge inside of those agreements that doesn't just amount to looking at "page 26 of a poor PDF copy." And when you're a business such as ours … and contracts are important for every business … but when a business, such as Accor's entire market value, is effectively driven by the IP in the contracts that we have … it's pretty easy to justify a CLM. However, our expectations for the CLM went beyond agreement management. We are a distributed business and Legal isn't centralized. We thought CLM could change the way we work, increase efficiency, and speed things up. Our expectations were high for what a CLM would deliver.

Well, all sounds rosy, right? Superprofitable business where contracts are deemed critical, a CLM system was acquired, and implementation began. Well, things got challenging ... quickly. Gathering the executed agreements was a yeoman job, but it got done. There were thousands of documents, but the organization stepped up and found (most of) them. Then the "metadata extraction" challenge began: a familiar trope for any company that has tried to create a contracts repository with metadata extracted, for search, retrieval, obligation management, and reporting/analytics—the overindulgence of metadata fields. In the case of Accor, the distributed organization felt it needed 350 metadata fields extracted from a typical 100-page agreement. Donald felt that "90% of these were duplicative, or could be obtained another way, or were simply not of business importance."

However, Donald and his team did indulge the requests, engaged a service provider to extract the metadata into the CLM repository, and paid a lot of money (well, they had the cash, right?) to get the job done. They had a repository! Whew. Onward.

Not so fast! Remember, the company had grand expectations to use the CLM to reengineer its contracting business processes globally. It selected one of the most business-critical agreements as a starting place and endeavored to configure the workflow while reengineering the process midflight. Donald described the expectations as follows:

> We were wowed by the ability to perhaps just create digital workflows and save all this legal time. So you know what, James, you need a new agreement for a hotel in Timbuktu, then just type in a few things here, and bang!—you've got a 100-page management agreement ready to go to the other side to negotiate, and then you could negotiate it right in the platform, and it'll be easy, and it will cut the time by two-thirds, and you'll save all this time and money. I think we were seduced by that [vision] as an organization, but what we didn't have, is that we didn't have the basic ground game in

place, and the systematic processes and alignment in place to deliver that.

So, Accor dreamed big. Not a capital offense by any stretch. However, there was another issue. Unfortunately, it had acquired a CLM software platform where the company behaved more like a vendor than a partner. The workflow configuration was unwieldy, Accor had to go back to the CLM software company for every little change, there was no ability to self-determine and configure the system on its own, and things started getting tense.

> This is where the overambition was, and part of the problems we then started facing were that when we started looking at CLMs and you start looking at the market in 2019 at least, there was a lot of salesmanship. Let's just be totally honest here. There's a lot of salesmanship that goes on, and people can promise a lot, and perhaps overpromise in terms of what their systems can deliver.

Donald faced a situation where he had supported the acquisition of a CLM system where the vendor overpromised and underdelivered, the contract repository was too complex, and the company didn't have policies and processes in place to compensate for the lack of functionality in the CLM system. Donald needed to "rip and replace" the CLM system.

Channeling either Abraham Maslow or Abraham Kaplan, depending on one's preference, "if the only tool you have is a hammer, it is tempting to treat everything as if it were a nail"—and Donald most certainly had a hammer. Accor in 2022 had generated 4.2 billion Euros in revenue; EBITDA (earnings before interest, taxes, depreciation, and amortization) of 675 million Euros; and hundreds of million Euros of free cash flow. Contracts were critical to these results. His hammer was obvious. Add to this the fact that Donald was senior, well-respected, accomplished, and had the legal training and imprimatur to walk into the CEO's office and say, "We need to replace our CLM system." He didn't wield the hammer. Instead, Donald took the exact opposite approach: finesse vs. brute force.

> We focused on getting a lot of stakeholder engagement from different parts of the business early on, and because the way that we had captured all this data became important for the business, everyone was onboard. Then when we created a repository, we already had a win in the sense that we had already achieved something big that we didn't have before.
>
> And then we were very honest, and we said, "Look, we have ambitions to do X, Y, Z, and those ambitions, we think, would be better met by considering a switch of the CLM platform." And that's ultimately how we socialized the need for a change, and we spoke to a lot of different departments saying, "If we could do this, would that be helpful?"
>
> Usually we picked questions where the answer would be yes, and so that allowed people to buy in saying, "Oh, yes, well that seems great, and if you can't do that with the existing platform, or it's not optimal to do that with the existing platform … then sure, I support a change."
>
> It gets people onboard early to have a bit of alignment in sort of thinking about moving that platform. So I think we were very lucky.
>
> We also created a series of legal champions across the world who accepted talking to me and who extolled the benefits of what the system can bring.
>
> There's a massive change management thing in any organization that goes on where people have a way of working and people don't really like change. Ultimately, there's a psychological element of it. It's difficult to embrace different things, but if you show the possibility of something, you get people excited and you bring them in early—I think it really pays dividends in terms of getting them to help you through that difficult process of switching a platform.

Donald didn't have to do this work. As noted, he had a hammer and could have used it. However, he didn't. He knew that for any change or program to sustain itself, it needed humans involved in the program to buy in. Nothing could be done by fiat. And if you ever meet Donald (I sure hope you do), you will know that he is not the type of person to wield a power hammer.

This cautionary tale is poignant. We feel that as Legal Ops gains traction and credibility in an organization, there may be a temptation to rely on previous wins and "cash in" on one's personal political capital. Donald's story is instructive in that, even if one can brute-force something, there is much more sustainability and yes ... empathy (see Chapters 6 and 7) in employing finesse.

Speed Bumps on the Road to Success

Those who are new to GenO can thank those who have blazed the trail for pointing out many of the hazards they encountered along the way. Building strong peer-to-peer and mentor relationships with these veterans through such organizations as the Corporate Legal Operations Consortium (CLOC) can help GenO aspirants get where they want to go with fewer speed bumps. But as part of an emerging profession, we should not expect an obstacle-free ride.

The evolution of the Legal Operations role is being ushered in as we speak. We are redefining the role of Legal Operations. As we've explored in previous chapters, GenO is keen to find a business problem and solve it. GenO is incredibly proactive. The role has evolved into a complex remit—a role that is multidimensional. It's not just ideas, it's concrete value-addition potential.

LegalOps.com's Connie Brenton has been part of this evolution. She was there in the early, formative days. She experienced the frustrations and failures. She passes on the wisdom as well as the cautionary tales. Now, she bears witness to the emergence of a new profession.

The General Counsel way back when was a figurehead. It was somebody who didn't have the wherewithal to make it in private practice, so they'd put them in there and they would manage outside counsel. We are a far cry from that now. Now the General Counsel are considered a business partner, with Legal Operations knitting the process together across the corporation. Many General Counsel are moving into strategy roles and CEO roles, with a tight interdependence on Legal Ops. It is the era of GenO.

And now our journey takes us to the future of GenO, and a bright one it is.

10

Predictions—the Next 5 to 10 years

I have seen the future of Legal Ops, and I know that in the coming months and years, we will witness a massive shift in our industry. Every one of us will have to transform actively. I cannot wait.[1]

JENN McCARRON, President, Board of Directors, Corporate Legal Operations Consortium, April 2024

Can Jenn McCarron see into the future? Some may believe she can … there are times when we think she has superpowers. Whether one believes this or not, McCarron has had the opportunity to build her career in Legal Operations from a unique vantage point.

She initially built her Legal Ops chops at Tandberg, a leader in videoconferencing that was eventually acquired by Cisco. At Tandberg she built out contract management and document management business processes, directly supported by the General Counsel. When Cisco acquired Tandberg, McCarron focused on merger integration of Tandberg's contracting processes with Cisco.

At Cisco, McCarron met Steve Harmon. We have already noted that Harmon has taught many of today's GenO leaders the Legal Ops craft. McCarron is one who benefited from Harmon's tutelage. After five years at Cisco, McCarron led Legal Technology for Spotify for almost two years, then was recruited by Netflix

---

1. Jenn McCarron, "I Know the Future of Legal Ops. Welcome to the Space Age," LinkedIn.com (April 15, 2024), https://www.linkedin.com/pulse/i-know-future-legal-ops-welcome-space-age-jenn-mccarron-cq5wc.

to build and lead the Legal Ops function. She did this for more than five years and then was appointed President of the Board of Directors of the Corporate Legal Operations Consortium (CLOC). Unique vantage point? We think ... yes!

The question isn't "Do we agree with McCarron that the Legal Ops profession will see a massive shift?" Rather, it is "*Why* do we believe she's right?"

Inevitability Born from Precedent

Legal Ops initially took form outside the law department when Legal needed technology and process support. The Information Technology departments of companies appointed technologists to support Legal; procurement departments appointed liaisons who could support interactions between Procurement and Legal (in particular when it came to contracting). Program management offices of companies appointed experts to interface with Legal as the legal department's involvement in enterprise initiatives grew. As Legal spending grew, Finance departments appointed Finance Planning and Analysis (FPA) experts to help with Legal budgeting. Compliance departments broke away from Legal as regulators wanted standalone groups focused on compliance and reporting. These groups also had liaisons who interfaced with the legal department. Similarly, HR/People departments either had legal experts on staff or interacted with Legal daily to ensure compliance with the rapidly changing employment law landscape. No group was untouched by Legal, and all interactions had a process or risk management or technology element—or often all of the above.

The office of the General Counsel in most organizations has moved beyond a mere support function with internal customers (OK, yes, this is one of the core missions, but ...) and is now viewed as an integral business partner in strategic decision-making. As chronicled in *The Generalist Counsel*, this trend really picked up steam about fifteen years ago when General Counsel were catapulted onto the core leadership team, no longer under the wing of the CFO.

There was precedent for this if one follows the path of the CIO.

> Over the past three decades, the Chief Information Officer in the corporation has evolved from being the steward of the company's IT infrastructure to the steward of company data to the steward of company information and company knowledge. "CIOs will need to master four emerging personas in order to compete in the new environment—Chief Infrastructure Officer, Chief Integration Officer, Chief Intelligence Officer and Chief Innovation Officer." This evolution is very similar to the evolution of the role of the General Counsel and is also the driver behind the need to incorporate knowledge of technology as a key dimension of their charter.[2]

As outlined in previous chapters, we believe that the new stature of the GC is the result not only of their own imprimatur and influence but also because Legal Operations enabled the GC to overtly show the leadership team that there was value to a legal department.

None of that has changed, and, in fact, the interdependence between the GC and Legal Ops has only increased in intensity. Therefore, two key factors that will continue to fuel the rise of Legal Operations are the continued rise of the legal department as "glue" to hold together enterprise business processes and the continued prominence of the General Counsel as a true business executive. General Counsel have already demonstrated that they can occupy the CEO seat, but we will see in the next five to ten years this trend continuing at an increased pace. Legal Ops will mirror this trend.

---

2. Prashant Dubey and Eva Kripalani, *The Generalist Counsel: How Leading General Counsel Are Shaping Tomorrow's Companies* (New York: Oxford University Press, 2013), 123; Kristin Burnham, "4 Personas of the Next-Generation CIO," cio.com (March 2, 2011), https://www.cio.com/article/282470/it-strategy-4-personas-of-the-next-generation-cio.html.

Risk-Adjusted Value Creation Will Supercharge Legal Ops

There is a continued need for organizations to balance risk and value. Value creation in organizations will be surrounded by greater expectations of precision and integrity given the pace at which technological innovation continues to evolve.

Let's take for example contract management as an enterprise initiative. Initially, contract lifecycle management (CLM), when driven by the legal department, was focused on intra-legal-departmental efficiency initiatives. How can we draft contracts faster? How can we review and negotiate contracts in a more standard way where business-as-usual contracts are done in a more automated fashion, and we can enable lawyers to practice more law by focusing on higher-value, higher-risk contracts? This is still a key focus area; however, companies have realized that the value contained within contracts and contracting business processes can be extracted to make better business decisions outside of the construct of the contracting business process.

For example, CFOs are now asking questions such as "Can I do dynamic revenue recognition consistent with ASC 606 using the data around pricing and terms in our contracts integrated with our enterprise resource planning systems?" This type of value creation is not something that was contemplated as a possibility just two to three years ago. However, the advancement of technology; the availability of data; the growth of data warehouses and data lakes; and, of course, artificial intelligence have all converged to throw the contracting business process into the epicenter of value creation. Legal Operations has been the key lever that has driven these initiatives, as the CFO looks to the General Counsel to help them answer these questions.

General Counsel will inevitably look to their Legal Operations leaders to "turn these (CFO) aspirations into action." The contract management value creation opportunities described above are a small example of myriad opportunities where Legal Operations can play a critical part. Of course, the risk/value balance comes in when we think about things such as data integrity. In order to support something as critical as revenue recognition analytics, Legal Operations needs to ensure that the repository of information they maintain has high integrity. This is where risk management comes in. How do they provide value to the CFO while ensuring that they don't encumber the organization and bring it to its knees in creating and maintaining this contract repository? Something that was seemingly tactical in the past has become tremendously strategic. How can they leverage artificial intelligence in order to speed up the process? How risky is the use of AI? To what extent do they insert humans in the loop in the process to maximize efficiency but also minimize risk? Legal Ops is perfectly suited to solve problems such as this and capture associated opportunities. And all of this is yet more evidence of the criticality of Legal Ops in an organization. GenO is real.

OK, OK, Let's Talk About AI

We resisted the temptation to make this book all about AI. That's because AI is part of the story (a big part), but not the whole story. The use of artificial intelligence by Legal Operations is not new. Traditional AI has been used by Legal Ops for at least a decade to extract metadata from contract documents and to support e-discovery document review and legal knowledge management. With the introduction of generative AI, the calculus has changed. The opportunities that are presented to Legal Ops to further supercharge efficiency and ensure they are "supplementing humans, not supplanting humans" are incalculable.

The More Things Change, the More They … Change

The most fascinating thing about the adoption of AI in legal departments and used by Legal Ops to support the corporation is that it is generally following the same curve as other legal technologies. However, the pace at which generative AI is being adopted is dramatically faster. The reason behind this is that experimentation and results have a much faster cycle than other technology disruptions. It takes a mere few days to do things such as create a bespoke clause using generative AI that is responsive to a red line in a contract coming back from a counterparty, run it through a quick review, and make it a permanent part of a negotiation clause library. In the past, this process would have taken months.

As the regulatory environment changes, Legal Ops is able to use AI to identify a change in regulations in partnership with their colleagues in finance, compliance, data privacy, and HR, and identify which contracts need to be remediated if a particular clause is missing or needs to be amended. Then with a few key generative AI prompts, Legal Ops can create an amendment that incorporates new language and kick off a workflow to send it out to the counterparty for signature. This identification, remediation, and repapering process would have taken months, if not years, and hundreds of thousands of dollars and large teams. The degree of (productive) disruption enabled by AI is again something that Legal Ops is perfectly positioned to lead, and, in fact, corporate leaders will look to Legal Ops as their first stopping point to drive initiatives such as this. The value creation inherent in something like this is obvious. Did Jenn McCarron see this in the future of Legal Ops? We certainly do.

When we asked Donovan Bell, Director of Information and Contract Experience (Global Legal Operations) for Intel Corporation, to just break it down into "primary colors and large numbers" (Bell is masterful at making the complex understandable), here is what he said:

> We use our systems and our tools to hopefully automate, streamline, simplify. So rather than me having to go into a system, log in, do this and that, I see a note on my phone and I can

click a button and now I've approved a request/action/contract, and it's out of my hands into the next person's hands ... from a workflow automation perspective. Much simpler, much more streamlined. [The effectiveness of AI is in] finding those small, low-hanging fruit pieces that I kind of look for. And then having those broader conversations of how we can also maximize [decison-making] assistance to humans using AI? That type of approach is critical. Simply the problem and simplify the solution ... for humans.

Being able to find information quickly, being able to decipher a scenario ... acknowledging that there are some unique situations—but focusing on the basics such as where can I find that data and information quickly? And so again, kind of streamlining some low-hanging fruit processes, but also being able to simply find the information in a seamless way. We have to also look at this from a standpoint of clean data. I don't think that there's a lost investment in ensuring that your data is clean and accurate so that you can clearly categorize and operate when you're trying to innovate.

And so if you're able to do that and take the time, even if it takes a chunk of time to do that, it's a wise investment because if your data's clean, it makes things a whole lot easier. The power of AI lies in simple workflows for simplified problems and high-integrity data that you have spent the effort to ensure is clean. That's what human-centered processes need.

Bell is a quintessential example of the new cohort of GenO Legal Ops professionals who understand the human centricity of all we do. We have already discussed the importance of blending data centricity and human centricity, and Bell's description of scenarios above perfectly depicts how GenO leaders will continue to be in demand in organizations that value pragmatic approaches to leverage AI and make a real impact in companies.

Ethics As the Foundation of Integrity—Legal Ops As Steward

Of course, no conversation about AI can be complete without Legal's role as the ethics steward. As conversations about responsible use of AI become more active in organizations, the office of the General Counsel is again thrust into the midst of these discussions. It's not just about ethics, it's about following the law, which ironically is in flux because AI is changing daily. Is Legal Ops well-positioned to build and rebuild a plane in midflight? Of course. Legal Ops does this daily. As such, will General Counsel rely on Legal Ops to support the operationalization of any policies and processes that put guardrails around how AI is used responsibly in organizations? We believe yes.

Let's Go Back to the Humans

As described previously, GenO professionals need to employ power (soft) skills in conjunction with technical (hard) skills in order to make impactful change. We can't overstate the importance of this. The roots of this profession are in technical and process and data-centric domains. However, as organizations have internalized themselves as living organisms where the value of humans is reinforced daily (remember when the transition from Chief Human Resources Officer to Chief People Officer began?), Legal Ops' success has been directly driven by their ability to blend data and human centricity in all they do.

The most successful GenO professionals take a "collaborate and control" vs. a "command and control" approach; favor "iteration over big bang"; value metrics and measurement but realize that management gut feel is also of value. As the profession has grown, finesse has overtaken brute force and nothing is ever accomplished by fiat. Legal Ops has become masterful at making a business case to executives and garnering the allocation of significant amounts of financial resources to support the initiatives they champion. GeoO realizes AI exists to supplement, not supplant, humans, and almost all processes powered by AI need to go through a "human in the loop" validation. We see the future being fundamentally human, and GenO Legal Ops has masterfully transitioned from a "hard science" domain to one that leverages the hard sciences to make a real impact on humans.

If You Want to Go Fast, Go Alone. If You Want to Go Far …

All of the reasons we have outlined above for why GenO Legal Ops are nowhere close to the end of their eventual destiny are valid. However, the most powerful dynamic that will propel this profession forward is that the GenO community rarely suffers from loneliness. Here's what we mean.

If an aspiring GenO Legal Ops professional wants to learn from those who have carved pathways before them, all they have to do is drop them a LinkedIn invite or reach out via the CLOC community site or just email someone. The community will respond.

If a GenO professional presents at a conference and shares tools, tips, and takeaways, they are always willing to talk to attendees afterward and give them more specifics. We have observed friendships and mentor-mentee relationships form in real time, right after an attendee walks up to a presenter. The willingness to share without fear of competition is a unique dynamic of this community.

The "community" is also very broad and inclusive. Knowledge flows freely between practitioners and providers; professors and pundits; students and stalwarts. No knowledge source is disrespected, and all views are indulged. We have seen practitioners transition to provider and back to practitioner. The boundaries of what a Legal Ops professional can do on their pathway to GenO are limitless.

If a Legal Ops professional is struggling personally, they turn to the community and the community responds. No one is ignored. No turmoil is too small to seek help from the community. Stories of struggle and glory are shared without fear of judgment, and shared pain and shared joy are in abundance.

If this seems too "soft" to be what we consider a powerful growth accelerant, just look at the growth of the Corporate Legal Operations Consortium from hundreds to more than 6,000 in eight short years. Conferences now have attendees that span multiple generations of Legal Ops professionals. Virtual forums are in the hundreds. If one wants knowledge of "what to do and how to do it," it's just a few mouse-clicks away. The collaboration without competition dynamic we described above is, in large part, due to the foundation created by CLOC. Collaboration and community have been inextricably linked from Day 1 of CLOC, and that ethos has only become stronger as the community has grown in number.

We feel that this community and collaboration dynamic is unique in kind. It has existed elsewhere but not in the way that it manifests in Legal Ops. As we profiled the GenO professionals in this book who shared their successes, vulnerabilities, and aspirations, it became clear that they were at the top rungs of their career ladders and about to crawl over the top. It was also clear that all of them had reached down to pull others up. No one has pulled the ladder up behind them. This "help others" dynamic is not unique to Legal Ops, but it is a foundational attribute that rises above others. The community collaborates and celebrates each other.

We, the co-authors of this book, are living examples of this dynamic. One is a tenured lawyer and senior Legal Ops executive in one of the most widely heralded household-name companies in the world. The other is a consultant, serial entrepreneur, high-tech business executive, and provider of technology and services to the legal community. Yet we have come together with a shared vision, shared ideas, and shared aspirations. We have collaborated with one goal—to endeavor to add value in our small way to the community we have chosen as our own. We couldn't be more different, but, then again, we couldn't be more similar.

We hope that you have enjoyed reading this book as much as we have enjoyed writing and producing it. We believe the full potential of Legal Ops is yet to be realized, and we hope that the stories we have shared with you are in some small way inspirational—or, at the very least—cathartic.

Peace

Contributors

Insight and experiences of the following individuals, to whom the authors are deeply indebted, formed the backbone of this book:

LUCY BASSLI
founder and principal
InnoLaw Group, PLLC

DONOVAN BELL
Director of Information and Contract Experience (Global Legal Operations)
Intel Corporation

PETER BRAGDON
Executive Vice President, Chief Administrative Officer, General Counsel
Columbia Sportswear Company

CONNIE BRENTON
founder and CEO
LegalOps.com

STEPH COREY
CEO and co-founder
UpLevel Ops

CARRICK CRAIG
Senior Counsel
Miller Canfield

JAMES DONALD
General Counsel, Regional Support and Legal Operation
Accor

LOURDES M. FUENTES
founder
Karta Legal, LLC

SALLY GUYER
Global Chief Executive Officer
World Commerce & Contracting

STEVE HARMON
COO and General Counsel, *Elevate*
Co-Founder, *Corporate Legal Operations Consortium*

JEFF KINDLER
CEO
Centrexion Therapeutics Corporation

JENN McCARRON
President, Board of Directors
Corporate Legal Operations *Consortium*

KYLE MCNEIL
Contracts Lifecycle Management Practice Leader
EY Law

BOB MIGNANELLI
VP, Legal Strategy/Operations, Digital & Technology, & Procurement
Haleon

CAITLIN MOON
Director of Innovation Design, Program on Law & Innovation
Vanderbilt University Law School

MARY O'CARROLL
Chief Operating Officer
Goodwin

TOM SABATINO
Executive Vice President and Chief Legal Officer
Rite Aid

RUBY SHELLAWAY
Vice Chancellor, General Counsel, and University Secretary
Vanderbilt University

LIZZIE SHILLIAM
Chief of Staff and Legal Operations, Office of the General Counsel
Vanderbilt University

TOMMIE TAVARES-FERREIRA
Senior Director, Head of Legal Operations
Cedar Cares, Inc.

CHRISTINE URI
founder
ESG for In-House Counsel

GERALD WRIGHT
retired leader of the Global Contract Solutions Group
Intel Corporation

Printed in Great Britain
by Amazon